Poetry Pages

A Collection of Voices

From Around the World

Volume III

Poetry Pages:
A Collection of Voices From Around the World Volume III

ISBN: 0-9768076-1-0

Poetry Pages Is...

A Cheshire's smile
An Alchemist's phial
A Satyr's leer
An ode to a beer
The symmetry of space
A father saying grace
The language of tangerine
A unicorn figurine
A Stradivarius violin
A thousand angels on the head of a pin
A moth fluttering by candlelight
A mother's crooning to a babe at night
A teardrop fraught with sorrow blinking
A man whose island's slowly sinking
A conversation within a dream
A distraught woman's silent scream
An overdose of painful afflictions
A message of hope in a spiritual prescription
A sonnet that captures a jaded eye
A remembrance of innocence asking "why"
A tale that makes us feel at home
The sorrow of loss and being alone
A collection of words gathered in books
An addiction to songs with soulful hooks
A Haiku written without a verb
The warmth of a hug in a chosen word
A phallic invasion of paper with pen
The indigo droplets ejaculated within
A lover's letter tossed into a fire
A poet inflamed with naked desire
A seeker reaching beyond the veil
The block that torments the writers who fail
The ones who leave when writings a hassle
The ones who remain to taste Eden's apple
The rose that blooms on a bed of thorn

A poet may bleed but his blood runs warm
These Poetry Pages you won't soon forget
Nor those beings being beings on the net
The streets of heaven or the chambers of hell
The places that poets know only too well
A promise we make while here we do dwell..
We'll meet you there if you've a poem to tell

Dennis R. Schmunk (Eternum 1)

"PoetryPages.com is a wonderfully unique meeting place, where friends from all over the world can come together and communicate with each other.. it always feels like I'm among friends when I'm there. The talent, as well as the helpful kind encouragement that I've found there, have made PoetryPages.com a very real and important part of my life."

Valarie Vandegriff (moonflower)

"The Familia means the world to me... I joined at a time when I really needed some support and friendly shoulders... and all the members have been so kind... They know the real me and still like me... and can bring a smile to any teary eyed face within a flash... To each and every Poetry Pages member, I thank you for your love and support."

Naushin Walji (friend_forever)

Table of Contents

Dennis Schmunk (Eternum 1) 181

Lamarr Smith (foreverflame) 201

Rabab Ahmed (buttterflies)

New York, USA

I was born in 1981 in Bangladesh, my home away from New York. The many wandering years in between have brought me to my current position of pursuing a Masters Degree in English at Rutgers University. Writing is more than a hobby for me; it has become a perspective on life. I write about all I see around me; everything from love, death, nature and culture to aspects of life that either suffuse us with inexplicable joy or leave us speechless at the inhumanity that surrounds.

Lampposts & Colors

ever notice streetlamps
just at dusk,
suddenly lit red,
glowing angry
and loud.

ever notice clouds
before a storm,
gathering
descending,
yet never quite reaching.

ever notice trees
bent double
in a breeze,
windswept, unheard,
screaming their tales.

ever notice crickets
chirping away
into darkness,
thousands of stories,
none comprehensible.

ever notice love,
unrequited in eyes,
beacons of devotion
as they glance,
shimmering with want,
behind the beloved's back.

Upon A Lily Pad

I was left twirling on a lily pad
watching the world drift away
the waves shook beneath me
around me, leaves blew astray

The brittle winds they hailed me,
I sat, crowned with jewels of dew
watching blue jays dance about
green of water mixing with their blue

I sat upon my solitary throne
and watched the world fade away
the banks of the lake whispered
the bamboo begged me to stay

I was abandoned on a lily pad
as the world danced in flames
the fiery colors seethed at me
mocked, as I watched in vain

I was left twirling on a lily pad
my universe, flawless and round,
watching the world get farther
I heard it crying without a sound

And my lily pad it danced,
danced with mesmerizing gait
summer's silence enveloped me
enchanting my eyes while I wait

Peace

speak to me of Peace,
of Love and Unity,
of mankind as One
tell me Peace exists,
lend me some Hope.

'tis a dream, you say,
'tis fighting with words
'tis worth the bloodshed
'tis only Battles of old.

we're bleeding, we're crying,
screaming our hurts
but no one listens,
and we dry up, Trying.

i see this World in spectrum,
multicolored and Raw
people searing for Love,
but Hatred draws a fierce line.

barbed wire lines, etched,
separate our Colors,
separate me from Love,
what's the use of Religion,
if you burn the books,
if you strip away Love.

i see the bodies fallen,
lives caked and cracked,
i see their Souls, desperate,
showing us our follies,
wizened with Age.

don't tell me of Politics,
of Religion or Faith,
tell me of Humanity
of that which transcends;
of Love; that which Unites.

speak to me of Peace,
a World we can build,
mend these holes we created,
we'll stitch together, side by side,
and we'll create a tattered Peace.

Spine To Spine

beckon me   into you
my beloved,   my phantom,
synchronized,   indivisible minds
we lie together   beneath gold
fingers   touching
shoulders   gripping
each   other
we will   lie as
kisses   glide
skin   whispers
souls   entwined
soul mates   that we are
breathing in   monsoon sighs
watching quietly,   blinking together,
limitless green   of summer lights
feed our love,   destined forever,
angel wings   brushed as one
painted in red   as we lay below
spine   to   spine

Silver Spurs & Summer Wine

February comes and goes, January's died
thought I'd see you again soon sometime,
hoped you'd hold me again, tomorrow

April sings our melancholy tune,
broken-record dreams that we once held true

Come May & June, summer will bloom,
without you by my lonesome side

August brings autumn at its heels
your voice resonates the changing hues

Winter takes its first salty breaths,
blows its unlikely warmth my way

Where do I go now that I'm lonely
As the year begins again its chores,
and again I see blue eyes alone;
blue and alone.

Barren Serenity

One-thirty in the afternoon and I wait
utterly uninspired, hoping for a break
They sit next to me, engrossed in each other
winds swoon about them, unseen
...and the bench grows colder

They shiver, they hold on tightly,
and I sit alone, petrifying,
look at these blank lines, hoping for hope
Next to me, a man in dark glasses exhales
...and I wait for inspiration

He reads his paper, brittle and ashy,
he hums a tune, incomprehensible,
cryptic notes tangled up in cold lips
The couple laughs, they kiss
...my pages remain dry, wanting

The lady with the sparkling shoes,
diamonds in her fingers and eyes
going to work late, her husband rings,
A dinner date awaits her beyond
...my toes begin to freeze

The trees grown dark and languid,
winter's touch painted a pretty ice,
birds and beasts in slate-gray shades
Leaves turned their backs upon us
...and the roads grow weary

Love withered and buried below,
beneath six feet of sleep and sleet,
Frostbitten sighs of winter mornings
enhanced to bitter deluge of afternoons
Washed out, worn out, like an old shoe
...and the passengers wait for a sign...

Body Number 63

That one hazy afternoon
I was number two,
second best out on the field,
looking across the team,
our cricket team shone
bright in the afternoon sun

We heard distant rumbling,
the ocean breathing slowly,
felt the comfort of the day
roll to us in waves,
touched reassuring heat,
as our backs burned

My brother was number one,
the best we ever did see,
he ran faster than a gazelle
but that afternoon,
he couldn't run so fast

We heard the thunder
growling underneath us,
our cricket field rose,
awashed in blue,
I saw my brother's eyes
searching for me
and then we disappeared

I was number two back then,
my brother number one,
now I lie amid broken bodies,
in body bag "Number 63"
wish I could look around,
find my brother or my parents,
know which bag is his,
return to our afternoon again.

** In memory of the lives lost in the Tsunami of 2004 in Southeast Asia*

Fall of the Muse

Inspiration hits as leaves begin to fall,
succumbing to blasts of late summer.
Hot, sticky sweat of sunshine dries up,
leaving behind a chillness confined.

Like ice cubes gliding over sunbaked paths,
rolling off the tongue, dripping onto skin.
Cool trails of moistened passion drizzle down,
melting cubes of romance drain slowly away.

Beads of late afternoon dew hang in shrouds,
a veneer of words, desperate to form thoughts.
Shreds of coffee cup dreams, entangled and old,
wave goodbye to summer love as eyelashes bat anew.

Muses return from bath-house vacations,
sent back to work on decaying brains.
Air left behind heavy and hot with unfinished desires
upon copper bedsheets sprinkled with red leaves.

Thrust back onto a cooling autumn world,
unceremoniously jolted from hazy sleep,
bidden to collect dreams scattered by hasty minds,
replacing jigsaw puzzles broken unawares.

Inspiration hits as Fall crumbles from the sky,
sun retreats as degrees fall in showers.
Clutters of leaves crunch loudly underfoot;
as leaves become words, dreamed into being.

Beneath the Mango Tree

When we met many lifetimes ago,
you were me and I was yours
we swung on branches of mangoes
burdened with our joint weight.
The hours had swam by like vast oceans,
spread apart by staffs of wise men
uprooted us into a blistering embrace
and we had yet held onto each other;
held on for the days that hurriedly swept by.
A sickly sweet smell of wilted red roses
mingled with the sultry scent of mangoes
as we gazed into the blurred distance
with fireflies weeping in our lost eyes.
When we had cried together, those days
wrenched us from each other's life,
breathed new souls into you and me
and we choked with ambition and pride.
We suffocated with the new minds,
the alien bodies we were then given
and I ceased to be yours, and you mine.
Now stranger, do you see me smile,
if we met again beneath the mango tree
will you recognize what I once was-- you?

Love Poem

Follow me, my love, into this abyss,
I'll scatter blood roses for your lips.
I'll string pearls into a pretty little noose,
we'll watch together the life you'll lose.

I'll decorate the bed with insect arms,
mesmerize you with my demonic charms.

I'll carve you a sculpture of human flesh,
give you new eyes made of clotted mesh.

Pay no mind to the voices you hear,
'tis only you and I, my love, so don't fear.
I'll bring you a bouquet of ivory bones,
to match with your skin's iridescent tones.

I'll trace the red away from your lips,
draw hearts on you with my scissors' tips.
I'll bring you gifts no other will ever give,
crimson slices for the moments you'll live.

I'll strew your path with angels' tears
petals of blood, to allay your fears.
Follow me into this hole underground,
my palace of death where you'll never be found.

I'll keep you safe, showered with love,
midnight upon you, no light from above.
I'll slowly gouge out your pretty eyes,
watch blood drip, drip, drip away the lies.

Your pain will be my sweet release,
my gift to you, to leave me in peace.

Castles in Our Eyes

Tell me a fable
of a time away from here;
where clocks have stopped,
an eternity at a glance,
where you make love from clay,
conforming under my fingers

Tell me of a place
bedecked with raindrops,
our lives cupped within;
where we sit and stare
into our images captured
inside beads upon our hands

Tell me of a love
hidden from prying eyes,
drenched in scented showers;
where we lie intertwined
let the breeze play over our lips,
sketch ourselves in the clouds

Tell me a fable
of a place in our dreams,
where our eyes interlace,
irises aligned perfectly,
this love contained in droplets;
where you & I remain us.

new phase of an old moon

his eyes blinked at me
captured me in their embrace
and i tumbled in headfirst
losing all feeling or sense

i tasted the love on his lips
a lingering desire spent
as he gazed at my disbelief
and smirked at my discontent

he bit my ears gently
nibbling on my fears
lowered his lips to my neck
dissolving the lost years

his whispers embalmed me
weaving me into a trance
trickled like a waterfall
their breaths miming a dance

i felt with my eyes closed
the kisses left by his smile
a muffled darkness drew me in
entangled we remained awhile

as our bodies slowly relaxed
with wistful smiles we sighed
the meeting of our fingertips
eclipsed the love we had tried to hide

Mortality's Vice

mortality screams,
opens its wary eye,
glances upon us
as we sit and wonder why.

blinks and retracts,
taking us away,
leaving behind a few
destined to see another day.

inevitably it draws,
further and closer in,
roads left to discover
places we've never been.

mortality comes,
unsheathing its claws,
plucking us like scabs,
one of nature's flaws.

Only for a Moment

When the world's barbarity stands out to us
bloody words seeping through the news
clotted red overcoming the black & white print
Our minds seize, stir, if only for a minute
the goosebumps on our arms rise in protest
If only for an instant, our lives revolt
wants to rear its shameful head and scream
Our sense of justice recoils
and we are ready to spar for peace
To suffer for the brothers we never played cricket with
To suffer for the sisters whose hands we never felt
With the parents whose love never touched us
We protest, we pervade, if only for a few breaths
and then the momentous chill subsides
Goosebumps fall back into their caves
our spines return to their curvature
and justice shrugs off its shoulders
The blood and betrayal we had forsaken
Only for a moment, we felt what it was
to feel the splatter of blood upon our faces
to see the crashed bodies intermingled
in a charred mess that was once definable
We almost knew what it was, to be lost.

words

in a darkened coffee shop
i waited for the servers to leave
sitting at my table, i dozed
with my eyes fixed upon you

jazz softly sang me a lullaby
and the words came dancing

spinning and twirling, they came,
while a single opaque light glinted

they weren't the words i knew
i stared at you, uncomprehending,
betwixt my half-closed eyes
i saw you nod and smile
and beckon me to sway,
through the haze of the room
the glasses tinkled and sang,
your notes caressed me
and extended a hand

the aroma of your kiss
mingled with the coffee,
wafted alongside the music
and paused breathless by me,
lending me a taste,
teasing my desire

the words you had said
rose in waves with the tune,
passed over me swiftly
in an undercurrent of love
and tugged me awake
to realize you had already gone

His Blue Shoes

He sauntered up to me slowly,
unlit cigarette dangling from his lips
a crooked smile upon his face
disarming me with its charm,
stared me up and down,
glanced down at his blue shoes
and asked me to dance

With a wistful desire I accepted,
put my fingers into his
and was twirled into the distance
He spun me swiftly around,
my feet barely touched ground.

We danced 'till the night waned,
felt the shivers of dawn greet us
as we melted into each other's arms,
our dance slowed its waltz
his fingers wavered by my hips

He whirled me in a dizzying spin,
a daring grin fixed within his eyes,
our dancing feet synchronized
with the meeting of our lips

With my bare feet planted firmly on his,
I danced another mystical dance
with the boy in the blue shoes.

11:11

a deja vu of time
moments replayed with precision
senses become aware
of time suspended
of emotions juggled

coffee grows stale
brewed again and again
same words spoken
laughter repeated
but between these eyes
i wonder where i had begun

every night the minutes stop
eleven eleven chimes
freezes and repeats
replaying images
like a movie screen broken

the same song plays
pauses with an exactness
rewinds and steps back
stops to ponder upon time
and i relive misery again
at eleven past eleven

What It Was

It wasn't the smile in your eyes
that captured my glance
It wasn't the perfect suavity you exude
that made me lean in closer
It wasn't the words you pretended to say
that mesmerized my thoughts
It wasn't the melancholy air you put on
that made me smile wistfully

It was the madness in your eyes
that drove me insane
It was the storm in your spirit
that shook me off this branch
It was the earthquake in your heart
that rattled the ground beneath my feet
It was the peculiarity of your smile
that made me feel I'm home

It was the familiarity of your obscurity
that swept me into love

Let Go

The beats in my head
fall in rhythm with the raindrops,
trying to outrun this screaming train
Grim, wet sky speaks aloud,
a silence of winter and rain
broken by the sobs of wooden tracks
as life slowly lets go--

Lost souls captured in each tiny drop,
racing the urgency of the wheels
The little boy next to me blinks,
his big brown eyes, opaque,
an endless depth of despair hidden,
collapsed lives ushered under waves
And the rain battles the day,
growing dark with sadness of little boys,
with the loneliness of fragile girls,
lost forever, trying to let go--

Dirty and drenched, the buildings droop,
church towers glisten with heretic tears,
The rain mourns the lost children,
the despondency we fight each day,
A solitary bird flits upon a black branch,
to cry upon, to nest upon, alone
and life lets go--

The train chugs along, so quietly,
battling with the static-y rain
Confused radio waves echoing laughter,
of joys shared in bygone days
A last stop, everyone alights,
I'm left staring into the eyes of the world,
only trying, trying to let go.

Julie Caldwell (Jaysie)

Chicago, Illinois USA

Unborn Sun

I will wrestle with the ghosts of loss
when mourning makes me wake
to find another morning persecuted
with an unborn sun
and razor sharp raindrops.

In a world devoid of Eden, I too
own one unborn son who is ever to remain
a reservation of unmeasured memories.
Rain splatters on the window
in an attempt to escape itself, but fails

the same way I do.

I am dry now, finally,
and faithless having been rewarded
with only pocket change and another day
of terrorist acid rain.
I am silenced by remembrance.

Circadian Addiction

I wonder what it's called,
this thing that forces
me out of my body-warmed
deathbed each morning.
It's some kind of sadistic,
circadian rhythm...
it must be the addiction
to tears.

Twinkle

His lines,
accentuated by the affections
of tree-strung white lights,
maintain my contours complacent
at his side.

The moon welcoming windows
are peering
enviously at the way we lay,
closely enfolded
and eye to eye.

I am singing to him softly
and he laughs
when my voice cracks and I know
I could repeat this scene
every Christmas Eve.

Three Days Awake

Sleepless
Mid-April night
His head rests on my chest
His quiet affords me no peace
In through the window the breath of dawn creeps
His lips feel weightless on my skin
His depression so deep
Three days awake
Sleepless

Passive

These days
of exquisite androgyny,
where we touch not to be felt
but only to feel
the reality of tactility,
grow longer, more idle
like this quieting autumn aura.
We smile without meaning
as we pass muted,
overused phrases.
We have become
only memories of lovers.

Illusion of Future

The eye-blue sky
is showing off
all of its seventy-six
degrees
as the barely-there breeze
brushes fragments of autumn
off of the sidewalk.
Yellows and reds are only
momentary,
mindless illusions
of future,
and for the moment
they are serving
to flavor this Indian summer.

Disillusioned

Last week's rain is settled
in the breaks of the pavement
as a liquid and stone collage
contorted below me,
as I step
outside of puddles.
A recollected white brick,
turned gutter-rusted yellow,
feels cold and damp
under my touch
even in today's blinding sun.
I round the structure, now
so much smaller
than I remember
to the side where the hedge line
used to divide
her yard from mine.
For years we had met there
to grow and pass notes.
The mulch and brush,
just like her house,
have long since been removed.
I turn back, beginning to understand
this part of the past
should only be revisited
in photographs.
This place no longer looks like home.

Haunted

Up
against
an army
of intrusive
little thoughts
that overbear
every strength
and weakness
this solo self
owns
and
as I
struggle
to disown
these so-called
memories
I wonder
why
Memory
is such
a haunting place
to be.

October

It was somewhere
within
the seventh
inning stretch
that I first found
brown
to be beautiful.
His eyes
reminded me
of something like
autumn
or nostalgia,
and I thought
to myself:
*if I remember
anything about today,
I hope it is
everything.*

Three-Fifteen

Two hours before dawn,
I cling to him as if he is
the very last source of heat
in a world that's void of light.
Amidst intertwined appendages,
we are drowsy, nestled deep,
within bruised and tattered sheets
that own heart-racing memories.

I Am

I am
an aesthetic addict
who is challenged by scansion.
I am Lutheran in practice,
but Buddhist by nature.
I place
my faith
in karma.

I know what is right
is not always best.
I'm a Taurus.
I'm stubborn.
I'm afraid to cry.
Barefoot, I am five foot nine.
I am thin – I have to be;
I am neurotic about weight.
I pop diet pills
and I never sleep.

I am pretty,
but I want to be prettier still.
I have big ears, but
I am not the best listener.
I am a fast talker
and a natural leader.
I love to be center stage.

I am the kissing-bandit,
a science nerd
and a National League fanatic.
I like to throw shoes
sometimes when I'm mad.
I am a serial dater and
I kiss guys with girlfriends.
I am wishy-washy

and lose interest easily.
I am eloquently undecided,
but I mean what I say.

I am punctual, dependable,
I follow through.
I am easily irritated
by those who do not.
I am sensual and sexual,
but not romantic.
I am always
waiting for winter.

I am unethical,
unpredictable and optimistic.
I am
the way
I have to be.

Newly Empty Rooms

Each night I linger
upon the prevailing shadows
that exhale
deep breaths
in newly empty rooms.

The moon
cannot find a bed post,
mirror or face
to reflect upon,
and so the darkness
multiplies and echoes
until the emptiness
is deafening.

Pastime

Footfalls
molded into the sand
aside the emerald marine.
The sea sighs,
sings
a rhythmic dirge
of forwards
and backwards.
Catch me if you can:
a favorite pastime
at home
in winds peppered with sand.
This amusement
relapsed
to an insistent longing,
still unsatisfied
and sticking to my skin
like a six a.m. April fog.
I wear it
while I walk the sea.
It seems fitting,
me missing you.

Here Again

He is so close
I can taste
the ways
he wears
the scents
of his hair.
Though we both know
it will lead to
the end of all things
(as we have never
been good at this)
I can do no more
than fall as snow.
I can only hope
the kisses are quick
and that the death
is slow.

Anarcha Erika Carter (GoddessErika)

Seattle, Washington USA

Reader, writer, and firm believer in passion, poetry, and prose- the Divine Trinity of language...

Death by Default

Pain searing
Blood seething-
Seeping from every orifice...
Carefully sharpened claws
Tearing,
Shredding,
Peeling away my soul.
Soaked in sweat,
Fear,
Tears I never knew
That I could cry.
You force yourself
Upon me-
Penetrate me,
Rape me
Of my world.
Reigning,
Blood staining,
Flaming
Gates of Hell...
Your Brutal
Barren hands
Asphyxiate me,
Inebriate me,
But refuse
To let me die.
Hollowed
And horrified,
Wretched
And writhing.
Restrained-
Chained to the stakes.
Pounded-
Driven through fists
Of rage.
Gnashing,

Slashing,
Piercing flesh
And grinding bone.
Your laughter
Licking,
Sticking,
Sickening my mind.
Wilted,
Tilted,
Guilted little girl...
Driven to,
Given to,
Death by default.

Hors d'Oeuvres

You lie there
In the palm of one's hand-
On display for all to admire.
They all "Ooh" and "Ahh,"
At how pretty you look
As they each take a piece of you-
A little sample to taste.
But that is all you are to them,
Just a pretty snack to chew on.
Then, once washed down
With a sip of champagne,
You are forgotten.

Sickened

I can feel it-
Somewhere deep within
An illness erupts.
Weak and sickened
I become.
Your venom permeates my blood.
Fragments of you
Still piercing
After all this time.
I always knew
You had a power
Over me,
Yet I failed to realize
Its potency-
Its toxicity
Until the cancer
Had already spread
Throughout my whole being.
I ache,
My limbs twitching at the numbness
That was once you.
Writhing and dizzy with delirium
I wait for death,
For the you that remains inside
To cease its existence
And leave what little is left
Of my heart
To beat to the rhythm
Of life-
Of my life
That you so nearly
Depraved me of.

Existence Filled With Shame

Tears shed as whispers
A voice rings in my mind
Words cut like razors
And again, I die inside.

As the shadows of yesterday
Slip between the cracks,
The light of what I used to be
Slowly dims, then fades to black.

Thoughts shot from broken arrows
Soar above these reddened skies
With piercing precision
They stab blindness in my eyes.

As I cry the years of tainted tears
That drip and bleed your name,
I drown myself in memories
Of an existence filled with shame.

Paper-cut Love With a Side of Lemons (a tanka)

Like a paper-cut
So swift and unexpected
My heart sliced in two
And then you return again
Pouring acid on my wounds

On the Shores of Castigation

Every hate ridden word
Every objection
That spills from your lips
Begins to puddle at my feet.
I watch the ripples in disbelief.
A new one forms
With every sickened curse.
Submersing my dignity
Drowning my worth
In your perverse pools of madness.
My trembling hands
Desperately search the darkness
For something-
Anything to cling to
But they find nothing.
The waters darken
As disgust forces me deeper
Suddenly I feel a calm
Then just before going under
I feel it-
The final blow of degradation
To my significance.

Your Head Hangs in Shame (a senryu)

You won't look at me
Fearing that I'll discover
The truth shining through

Second Guessing Sanity

I lean against the cold walls of nowhere,
Soaked skin
Another shiver from within.
I pass the time counting shadows-
Blackened images of who I've never been.
The skies grow darker
And I hold my breath
Trying to keep the heat.
A whisper barely audible
Grazes past my ears.
I feel a lump form in my throat.
Fear choked and frozen
I close my eyes-
Trying to pretend that I'm unseen-
Obscene
But comforting in thought.
I bury my head in my hands
Playing dead again.
Peeking through the tiny cracks between my fingers
I try to catch a glimpse
Of the voice,
But I see nothing.
Just another paranoid illusion to blame

The Truth (a tanka)

So, you asked for it...
Are you ready to listen?
Can you handle it-
Accept it for what it is?
Or will you refuse to hear?

Tick Tock... Tick Tock... In Envy Of The Clock

I watched the tiny hands of the clock
So graceful,
So persistent,
So determined to complete the day.
Never resting until the cycle-
The full circle is complete.
I envy whatever makes it tick.
I ache for an obsession such as that-
Always counting the ways
That such a passion
Would make my days so complete as well.
Yet no matter how hard I try,
I cannot harness even a fraction of its power.
Why I even ponder the possibility
I do not know.
I guess some things just weren't meant
To be equal-
Not meant to be so round.
I guess some things
Are not driven by the now.
Or maybe, some things
Simply aren't made to tick forever.

Suffocating Your Name (a tanka)

You gave me breath, life
But then you left me choking
On your hurtful words
Your name swelling on my tongue
Yet I can't bear to swallow

Thoughts From A Bowl Buried Deep In My Fridge

Spoiled rotten
Forgotten one.
Tucked away
Behind closed doors of darkness.
I condensate,
Rejuvenate,
Procreate some more.

This make-shift arctic wasteland
Incubates my spores.
The wretched stench of my decay
Strengthens more and more.

Watering eyes,
Luring flies…
'Til one day
Thrown away.

Goodbye My Dear Undying (an acrostic)

Moments lost
Instantly.
So unjustly your departure,
So sudden your absence,
I feel abandoned.
Numbed from endless days of
Grieving for you.

Your words echo
Over and over in my mind,
"Undying," you once said.

Solemnly I toss the flowers,
One by one upon your hallowed grave.

Arizona's Midnight

It's so quiet here without you
So dark, and so endless.
And though the sky above
Appears to be cooled by the night,
Her fiery twilight still very much remains
Hidden among the stars-
For this is Arizona's midnight.
I lie tucked beneath her sky
Patiently awaiting the sun,
Yet once again
The dawn eludes me.
What if forever never comes-
Never delivers you into my arms?
What will I do then?
Will the sun ever rise for me again,
Or will I disappear into the darkness-
Into the void of Arizona's midnight?

Unseen Savior

I walk with my hands in my pockets
Kicking up pebbles
Alone again on Rebels Road.

A familiar silence
Breaks in the distance
As your footsteps meet the ground.

"Is someone there?" I shout,
"Come out, come out
Wherever you are."

But I hear nothing,
Only singing echoes
So I continue on.

I shrug it off
As no big deal,
Yet I can feel your presence-

A certain safety
Washing over me,
Defending my existence.

Every path I beat
You loyally follow.
Every tomorrow you are there.

Dearest angel
I want to thank you
For guiding my way.

I pray that this finds you,
Wherever you are.
I unfold my fist
And blow a kiss into the wind.

Head in Your Hands (a senryu)

Tears wet with regret
His chapter comes to an end
And you're not in it

Dreamkeeper

Curtains wave across the foot of the bed
And I feel a faint chill run up my spine
Like invisible finger tips upon sleeping skin.

The shadows shift in the moonlight
Projecting nocturnal silhouettes
Translucent, yet lucid, on the wall.

A strange comfort tiptoes toward me
Unseen in the dim light
But somehow familiar nonetheless.

The curtains breathe outward again
And invite the night to enter.
Once more, the crisp air brushes by.

Rolling onto my side
I scan the room trying to make out
The ever shifting shape of the shadows.

Then suddenly, through the corner of my eye,
I see your face smiling back at me,
Watching over my dreams, as you always do.

The wind passes along one last whisper,
Pauses to leave its kisses on my cheek,
Then silently escapes into the darkness.

Flipping over, I return to my dreams
With skin smoothed and goose bumps gone,
My chills warmed over, and your subtle smile in my heart.

Hell Breeding Evil (an abecedarian)

Another
Babies'
Cry
Drowned out of
Existence.
Fragility
Given again to
Hates'
Incubation.
Jeopardize another life,
Kill another soul with
Lack of
Morals.
Nurture the
Oblivion.
Partake in the
Quest of
Reliving the
Sin.
Trapped inside
Unilateral lies.
Vortex of brimstone,
Wastelands you call home, so
Xerophilous
Your Torrid
Zone.

The Perfection That Is Us II (an acrostic)

So young, so naïve- I was
Everything you didn't need. My
Virgin body, my virgin mind would
Eventually be our demise.
No hard feelings, I just wasn't ready
To be whatever it was you needed then-
Even though I had wanted to,
Even though I had tried,
Naïvety took some time to heal.

Years passed 'til we met once more.
Excitedly we jumped right in again
Against the odds, and I was
Rediscovered and re-released
So quickly that

I abandoned all hope for our future,
Never giving it another chance

'Til now.
How love found us again so
Easily, I'll never know. I like to think that

Maybe, we were just meant to be
And we just didn't see it then, so we
Kept our distance; But
I'm here to tell you that I see it now.
Now I know... I am your other half, and I will never let you
Go again.

Even Without My Eyes I Know (an acrostic)

I saw you again last night-
Never mind that you did not see me.

Dreams are supposed to be like that-
Reclusive and mysterious...
Each of which you truly are,
At least in my mind anyhow.
Much like a wordless thought
Somehow spoken, yet left unsaid.

Invisible in my waking hour,

So vivid while I sleep.
Every detail of you becomes so clear that
Even without my eyes, I know that you are beautiful.

Lost & Found

Lost...
To prematurity
Born before its time
...The love of a little girl

Found...
Tucked away in the cellar of my soul
Aged like a fine merlot
Awaiting fates' toast to the future
... My love poured upon you

In Awe (a nonet)

In awe- I watched your shadow dancing
The candlelight upon your face
Mesmerized by your beauty
I traced your silhouette
Placed it in my mind
Tucked it away
My keepsake
Dancing
Flame

Under the Weather (a nonet)

Outside in the darkness I waited
Chilled to the bone and sopping wet
Dripping hair and falling tears
Indistinguishable
From one another
Consuming me
Drowning me
In your
Storm

Empty Heart Empty Hands (a nonet)

There was a time when I once held you
Right here in the palm of my hand
Yet somehow I let you slip
Right between my fingers
Now, I just stare at
The emptiness
And wonder
Where you've
Gone

Gillian Crawford (Gillian)

Ontario, Canada

Born in southern England and emigrated to Canada in 1969. Lover of all things art-ful.

Inside Outside Edge

Trying to keep my balance,
skittering across that
fine line you spoke of.

Narrow, golden thread separating
love and hate
madness and genius.

Skate that line, you said
and I would have
the best of both worlds.

The pain of your leaving
counterbalanced, against
the pleasure of your return.

Winter

Winter's interrupted
by glimpsing
spring's rehearsal

I Write Poetry

Perhaps an easier life
than Van Gogh, Serrat, Cassat
mortgaging house and home
sublimating hunger
for canvas, wooden palettes,
colours squeezed from tubes.

Dependent on morning, noon,
or evening light to
dictate brush-strokes.

I paint poetry
(only pen in hand)
piled-up sentences,
letters heaped
across a page
solitary self-portraits
made from words.

Encased

Summer dancing words
kept still in
icicled ink

Halfway

I'll meet you
halfway between

Allegro con brio and
Andante con moto.

I'll recall every overture you made.

After our champagne intermission
I'll watch his fingers
press down on black and white keys,
the only freedom from the starched black and white
that encases him.

I'll meet you
halfway between
Beethoven's deafness
and hearing Mozart.

Taste

If I'd never kissed
your fingers after
they found me,

I would never have
learned about
taste.

Hearing

When you separate
my lips,
spelling each letter
of my name
with your tongue
sliding between
vowel and consonant,
I hear the way
it was always meant
to be spoken.

Sight

Honeymoon
on and off between
snacking,
nibbling on
chips and salsa,
tongues melting milk
chocolate
squares
of sunlight
knocking on closed drapes,
half afraid of
seeing inside
each other
yet hungry for
its warmth

Touch

I can touch myself
imagining your hands
opening my body.

Opening scarlet, velvet petals
moistened by
your need.

Colour Blind

I've forgotten how
to mix primary colours.

What do I stir together
to change the saddest

Of blue to the colour
I see behind my closed

Eyes when your mouth
investigates soft purple

Petals, your tongue hardening
dormant roses.

Ice Wine

They call it 'Ice Wine',
fruit imperfect for harvest
until first heart,
then skin is frozen.

Sickly sweet liquid,
bottled in costly model-like
long necked,
anorexic bottles.

They say a smattering,
a scattering over ice-cream,
is the end
to a perfect meal.

Meeting

A psychologist he said,
poet too,
the blue-eyed
dark-haired
man I met last night.

Just something about
sapphire matched
with ebony
that I can't ignore,
or dismiss as coincidental
happenstance.

Sixth Sense

My mouth finds yours
before you ask.

Fingers travel, unmapped
across your body
knowing where you need
my touch.

It's different, every time
I begin this journey.

Showing you each corner
of yourself, uncharted,
map makers dream,
understanding

Where you start
and where I end.

Kimberly Drone (Kimmyjean)

Highland Park, New Jersey USA

I am married and have one son, 9 years old. I work as a Canvass Director for New Jersey Citizen Action. We are the largest "Watchdog" social justice coalition in the state. I have been writing poetry since the age of 14. I publish my own poetry web site and feature unknown poets to an array of graphics to help in advancing the art of writing. I dabble in graphics and web design as well.

Drink Of My Tears

Drink of my tears
Streaming within pain
Cascaded droplets
Reminiscent of rain

Swirled in a goblet
Imbibe amid its brine
Attested to sacrament
Risen for a shrine

Let their warm taste
Fill into your veins
Consumed in torment
Coupled in chains

Feel miasmic hazes
Submerge your mind
Stealthily throbbing
Until you go blind

Alter your reality
Integrate in my sorrow
Leaving your today
Entering my tomorrow

Drink of my tears
Streaming within pain
Cascaded droplets
Reminiscent of rain

Dance Across the Universe

Let's dance upon an edge
Of collective cosmos
Bounding towards
Untouchable stars
Journeying a tail
Of zooming comet
Sparkling amid
An evening sky

Let darkness surpass
Unto a wonder blush
Of shimmering sun
Upon our naked faces
As we embark
Unconstrained by
Human organization
Amid heaven's light

Waltzing throughout
Galilean Moons
Centered in motion
Upon Jupiter found
Dipping transversely
Into Cosmic rings
Of icy matter
Of Saturn bound

Plied our footstep
Encircled by femininity
Floating Ishta Terra
Of Venus mist
Rumba to a heat
Amid solar winds
Pulling in magnetism
Of Mercury warmth

Let's dance a cotillion
While transcending
In Sapphire radiance
Of beauty in Uranus
Holding each other
In a lover's embrace
In periphery of Pluto
Until foremost light

So let's dance across
Universal boundaries
Captivate in creation
Basking in genuineness
As we amalgamate
Into a singularity
Until we disperse
Never to be found

Luna's Mantra

Luna of extraordinary light
Regulator of good and right
Hear my mantra...
Hear my cry...

High above a sky of eve
Illumination spreads wanton beam
Minds unlocking its inner essence
Within an amalgamation of radiance
Feeding our vital karaka of life

Call unto your ancient myth of night
Bask us in shimmering light
Transcend your lunar rays
Augmenting our psychic maze

Surging controls of ebb and flow
Rippling within catatonic deluge
Spellbinding deep astuteness
Within water of our substance
Fluxing physics energies current

Send your invocation in words of rhyme
As we entreat into our divine
Release us to your shaman glow
Show unto us what we should know

Abashed in spirituality of night
Consuming enchantments of acumen
Basking amid silver moonbeams
Circled amid dualism of life and death
Entwined within its luminous power

Weave the knowledge of midnight hour
Enchanting me into precedent power
Surround me in a cycle of starlight
Cascade away all my inner fright

Luna of extraordinary light
Regulator of good and right
Hear my mantra...
Hear my cry...

Luna of Night...

Moon Child

Born in midnight hour
Deep within
Fortitude of night
Far away...
Inside a hallowed grotto
Entranced of mystic belief

Rays of incandescent blush
Swathed in luminous hue
Rising from waters
Of a elemental deep
Taking in her
...First breath
Crying her
...First cry

Skin prismatic amid
Luminescent blue
Tresses of ashen blaze
Orbed eyes of ebony night
Endowed by magick
Surrounded by charm

Existence begetting demise
Radiance begetting darkness
Arriving in a circle
Within Life
Sovereign of...
Astronomical deity

Raised in ritual clandestine
Frolicking within
Moonlight shine
Humanity bestowed with
Glimpses...
Of poetic divine

So in your journeys
Within pathways of eve
Listen in intent to hear
Chants that resonate
Of ancient time...
Amid illumination of
A great Sage's wisdom

Gaze...
As bewitching hour
Crosses lines of moment
Open your inner essence
And share....
Within an apparition...
Of a blessed
Moon Child

Moonlit Kisses

Touch your lips to mine
Transcendent of true divine
Sending me to heaven's light
Onto a realm within right

Moonlit kisses...
Butterfly whispers...

Serenade me below a moon
Captured within rapture tune
Cascading my internal mind
Beholding a treasure to find

Moonlit kisses...
Butterfly whispers...
Liberating my spirit
Within your mind

Trace your lips upon my nape
Shadowed amid darkness' cape
Emanating shivers down my spine
Savoring ecstasies outer brine

Moonlit kisses...
Butterfly whispers...

Place your hand upon my soul
Mystified within a grassy knoll
Illuminating upon my silken skin
Shadowing within deepest sin

Moonlit kisses...
Butterfly whispers...
Capturing my heart
Within your hand

Moonlit kisses...

Bride In Waiting

Separated from
Corporal structure
Gazing below....
Sight transfixed...
Darkened atmosphere
Surrounds...

Disparity flows
Emanating from
Lifeless structure
Tears unmoving
Within stillness
Amid swollen eyes

Silken tresses of gold
Fanned in grandeur
Laying upon a
White despoiled
Bridal gown

Inundated in blood
Surrounding...
Spreading...
Staining...
Upon a floor

Gathered within
Faultless arrangement
Posed in position
For photograph

An isolated
Creature shrouded
In ambiguity
Laying amid despondency
Solitary from life
Waiting for
Her Groom
To come home...

Soulless Eyes

She stands adjacent
A back dropped moon
Shimmering in a nocturnal haze

Dressed in black ebony silk
Clinging in sensuality
Each crevice of her formation
Blurring within
Apparition to behold

Her skin incandescent
Shaded within a pearly gray
Hauntingly stunning
Beckoning...
As she turns your way

Frozen in your step
Statuesque you stand
Hypnotized...
You wait...
Captivated in her eyes

Approaching your position
Slowly...
In waves of silk
Sashaying gently
In catatonic suggestion

Death's chill surrounds you
As you're transfixed
Within her glance
Empty orbs of oblique
Sparkle in romance

Surrounding you
Within her miasma of death
Breathing in her perfumed stench
You feel your blood
Slowly...
Begin to drain...

Drip...
Drop...
Tick...
Tock...
Upon the sands
Of a black clock

You look upon your hands
Saturated in wine-red
Coloring an argument below
Pulling your life from within
As she wafts your essence
Absorbing you into
Her soulless eyes

Naiveté's Rain

Heavens cry their abundant tears
As we stand misplaced in our fears
Streaming down to a ground below
Water abysses into what we know

Cry your sadness of naiveté's rain
Within sheets of angst, torment and pain
Amid a dark depression of internal din

Lonely souls crossing empty outlines
Into pathways that civilization refines
Flocking to a bright spoken pledge
Teetering upon sanities destitute edge

Cry your sadness of naiveté's rain...

Flooding an eternal vortex in remiss
Thoughts of eternity's path of bliss
Faced in our own false pretenses
As a misty haze begins to condense

Within sheets of angst, torment and pain...

Salted ocean waves of misery
Leading a life of internal debauchery
Conciliating our senses of good
Waning a life that's misunderstood

Amid a dark depression of internal din...

Caves of darkness prevail in dark water
Meeting a demon for their slaughter
Hungering for a illuminating light
Struck down in their lowly plight

Cry your sadness of naiveté's rain
Within sheets of angst, torment and pain
Amid a dark depression of internal din

Heavens cry their abundant tears
As we stand misplaced in our fears
Streaming down to a ground below
Water abysses into what we know

Twilight Magick

Twilight magick call unto me
Releasing my internal spirit
Setting me forever free...

Each glitter in the sky
Answers to my who what and why
Sing your songs of nighttime life
Take away my all my strife

As I dance under a magick moon
Contradicting daylight's break
Falling into an eternal swoon

Each glitter in the sky...
Answers to my who what and why

Sunset settles its brilliant tendrils
Within a exaltation of colors bright
Beckoning to an ever approaching twilight

Sing your songs of nighttime life
Take away all my strife...

Fragrances dipped in nighttime aromas
Cascade you in a mantra of elusive rhyme
Mesmerizing within a consignment of time

Luminous moon waves beckon and hypnotize
Cooling air bathes you within sundown bliss
Caressing you gently amid a nocturnal kiss

Crickets and owls begin creating harmonies
Easing you into a magick respite
As nightfall revolves turning amid a night

Each glitter in the sky...
Answers to my who what and why

Amethyst miasmas of midnight blue
Rolling elevated high above in a sky
Catching to a reflection deep in your eye

Sing your songs of nighttime life
Take away my all my strife...

Settling in a preordained reverberation
As we commemorate a sundown sacrament
Rocking you soothingly in contentment

Twilight magick call unto me
Releasing my internal spirit
Setting me forever free

Each glitter in the sky
Answers to my who what and why
Sing your songs of nighttime life
Take away my all my strife

As I dance under a magick moon
Contradicting daylights break
Falling into an eternal swoon

Breathless Whispers

Breathless whispers touch my skin
Slowly enticing me to feelings within
Caressing wings embraced in moment
Cradling you soothingly from behind

Rock me gently...
Rock me slowly...
Within a rhythm of double time
Slowly floating me into paradise of sublime

Leisurely tides of passion ebb and flow
Tenderly flowing in wraithlike glow

Bursts of luminosity fill my eyes
Passions spirit flowering in disguise
Bursting in multicolored collection
Warming of adoration's truest intent

Rock me gently...
Rock me slowly...
Within a melody singing its song
Elevating harmony's within a crescendo

The Land Of Unicorns

Take me to the land of mystic...
Where white unicorns stand pompous
Shrouded in hazing mists of lore
Representing virginity and chastity
In a chaotic world of immorality

Take me to the land of mystic...
Where hoof beats of unicorns
Fill up air with magical melodies
As silken manes flow to heavens
Painting kaleidoscopes of colors

Take me to the land of mystic...
Where unicorn form is luminous
Against back drop of universe
With off spring contiguous
As magical notes waft in air

Take me to the land of mystic...
As unicorns stand amid horizons
Essences of fairytale dreams
Of a hallucination like reality
Flowing through psyche

Take me to the land of mystic...
The Land of Unicorns

Bliss and Feathers

Send me to the edges
Of oceans bright and blue
Where sunsets surge in pledge
Colors shimmer amid diamonds
And romance of love is true

Embrace me among shrouds
Within silky flowing ivories
Covering our love within clouds
Uniting inside our spirituality
Told among fables and stories

Stretch me into a rainbow
Gliding within cascading slide
Transporting us in ebb and flow
In colorful sparkles sublime
On top of an epic romance ride

Share me in our rite of passage
As we grow mature together
Riding in a glittered carriage
Carried by stallions of white
Upon trails of bliss and feathers

Deborah R. Forest (Godspoetess)

Ontario, Canada

I'm a self-employed poet, composing poems for people, from my web site rosegardencollections.com. I am currently 55 years old and living in Ontario.

Ontario is where I was born and grew up. I began writing in August 1997. I've self published one book of spiritual poems called Rose Petals.

I joined the Poetry Pages January 11, 2004 and I'm proud to be part of the family here, reading their work and sharing mine with them also.

My Daddy

Dear God,
even though I'm a little girl
I'm curious about you,
One day I was told
you made the world including me too.

You made the flowers and butterflies,
the birds and the bees,
The tall grass growing in the fields,
and all of the trees.

The different colored fish
and the seas and oceans blue,
Along with my cat and dog,
they were made by only you.

You also made the sky
and the big yellow sun,
The moon and stars to shine
when the day was done.

You made everything in heaven too,
including the colorful rainbow,
That's why I was curious,
and its you I wanted to know.

I never had a daddy,
yet I was told you were my father,
I was so so excited
I went and told my mother.

Mommy never had an answer,
but knew exactly what to do,
She sent me to Sunday school,
where I could learn about you.

I ran across the field
every Sunday morning,
Each time I sat and listened
the more I was learning.

Sometimes it was confusing,
but before too long,
I found out who my daddy was,
and He was big and strong.

You're so big the world's your footstool,
and I never have to worry,
You love me so much,
and you're always watching me.

I cried when my teacher said
you were nailed to a cross,
And you died because
the people were so very lost.

I smiled once more,
because you came alive again,
And you forgave them,
and you're every body's friend.

When we are good you're happy,
but sometimes you are sad,
When the people you created
are acting terribly bad.

You don't like it when they lie or steal,
and make fun of your name,
But you will forgive them,
because you love them just the same.

I find it hard to understand God,
how some one as big as you,
Can make yourself small enough,
to fit inside of my heart too.

I'm not going to worry though,
I am so happy you're my daddy,
You love me more than anyone could,
and you're always here with me.

God's Beauty On Display

The sky is hazy with a hint of pink
as the sun begins to rise,
I hear jays calling for their treats,
before I rub my sleepy eyes.

Placing peanuts outside
on the railing one by one,
I'm glad to be up early and
greeting the morning sun.

Sitting by the window drinking a coffee,
I see a beautiful array,
Of multi colored birds,
eating food from my feeders on display.

In full view are several morning doves
scrounging for seeds on the ground,
While chippy scurries on by with,
a cheek full of nuts he has found.

Tiny yellow finches,
sparrows and chickadees too,
Are perched on a feeder
I placed by the window to view.

Busy blue jays
gather their peanuts eagerly all the while,
Their next direction is the feeders,
and I sit back and smile.

Silly red headed woodpecker
is senselessly,
Pecking on the roof of a tiny ranger station
I have hanging in the tree.

He's become a little wiser though;
sitting in an open feeder,
Feasting on sunflower seeds,
but prefers insects even better.

Bird baths with fresh water
entices my feathered friends I see,
As they take turns drinking and bathing
ever so happily.

Pesky blackbirds must have slept in,
or have flown somewhere faraway,
For they haven't shown up as of yet
on this most glorious day.

All and all its wonderful
waking up early to greet the day,
I can't imagine missing
Gods beauty on display.

(Oh my goodness, I can't help but say, this is so absurd,
I believe I've been fooled, I see some blackbirds)

Message In A Sparrows Song

Today a sparrow lighted
upon my window sill,
With its head held high,
bellowed out an awesome shrill.

It's song was a happy one
this strange morning in spring,
It was hard to believe because
today it was snowing.

The elements never deterred it
from singing its melodious song,
I was awe struck by it
I could have listened all day long.

Standing there glancing at him
through my window pane.
The snow kept on falling
and never once did he complain,

Here I was warm inside
with a roof over my head,
Asking God to stop the snow
and send the sunshine instead.

This tiny feathered creature,
looked up to the sky,
Singing to his creator,
as the bitter wind blew on by.

We complain about the weather,
and so many other things,
If only we were like the sparrow
and took the time to sing.

It doesn't matter what the weather
nor how big the storm,
Putting our trust in the Heavenly Father,
he'll keep us safe and warm.

When we're thankful
in whatever situations we find ourselves in,
Tis' when we find true happiness
and perfect peace within.

Complaining won't better it,
nor will it change a single thing,
But the trial will be much easier,
if we but learn to sing.

Today I thanked God for the sparrow
sitting on my window sill,
And for the message in a song,
He took the time to instill.

Love Through Mankind,
Reached Out To New Orleans.

The wind is howling the water raging,
people huddled together,
News reporters warned in plenty of time
about the nasty weather.

Many fled from their homes
for fear of the terrible storm,
They gathered their loved ones
taking them away from harm.

Back at home
in their familiar neighbor hood,
Are the unfortunate
who couldn't leave like they should.

Some climbed into attics and on roof tops,
as the water began to rise,
Others tied themselves together
trying to survive.

Many were caught unaware
as breeches came undone,
They climbed as high as they could,
there was no place to run.

With no means of transportation
to flee from their homes,
Full of fear and hopelessness,
they waited out the storm alone.

Elderly the disabled, young and old alike,
bowed their heads to pray,
That the storm would miss their dwelling place
and they'd be safe today.

New born babies and mothers,
the sick and elderly in hospital beds,
Closed their eyes and hoped,
none of them would end up dead.

Quickly the waters rose higher,
causing chaos and flooding,
Eighty percent of a city under water,
power goes out, and then there's the looting.

People in desperation, lives destroyed,
homes buried deep in cold merciless waters,
Panic fills the hearts,
children crying for their mothers and fathers.

Loved ones missing maybe dead,
the night is blacker than coal,
Screams are echoing into the night,
from the many weary souls.

Fleeing to the super dome
a shelter better than nothing else at all,
But hell was waiting inside,
and there was no one they could call.

Evil lurked in the shadows
taking advantage of the poor and weak,
While disease and illness began to surface,
it looked terribly bleak.

Time was of the essence,
but higher ups and officials weren't ready,
Adding more needless suffering and death
to the catastrophe.

Soon help came in the form of,
ordinary people with hearts from everywhere,
Opening their homes and giving finances,
water, food and clothes to wear.

Governments and leaders
began making strategic choices,
Because of caring people
who became the suffering citizens voices.

Just as they were losing hope,
of anyone coming to the rescue,
For the love of their fellow man,
the sun came shining through.

Know one will ever comprehend
this catastrophe or what it all means,
But each of us can relate to,
The Love Through Mankind,
that Reached Out To New Orleans.

A Flower
Called A Rose

The most beautiful flower
I suppose,
Is a flower called a rose.
Every year they bloom
in the warm summer sun,
Each rose a rare beauty
to everyone.
Their petals unfold
with grace and flare,
While their delicate fragrance
fills the air.

The most beautiful masterpiece
I believe to be,
Was when a cross
was made out of a tree.
Tis' where a Rose
of rare beauty one day,
Was nailed to a cross
to wash our sins away.
That beautiful Rose
hung there to die,
For a sinner
such as you and I.

The greatest act of love
I suppose,
When you shed your blood
you rare beautiful Rose
The Rose of Sharon,
a beauty to see,
Jesus a rare rose
He will forever be.

The most beautiful flower
I Know to be
Is a flower called Jesus,
the one who died for me.

The Garden She So Loved

Today I wandered off,
to a place of long ago,
Where butterflies and dragonflies
and bumblebees go.

I found busy ants and daddy long legs
scurrying here and there,
And a fragrance I can't forget
filled the warm summer air.

Bees were busy buzzing,
while birds were singing in a tree,
The sound of humming birds fluttering their wings
joined in harmony.

Lying there lazily on the ground
gazing up towards the sky,
I'm greeted on the nose by
a monarch butterfly.

My tummy shook from giggling,
I frightened it away,
It was fluttering all around
and seemed in disarray.

Striving to catch a busy ant,
I began to frown,
It drew the attention of the others,
and they were swarming all around.

Turning to walk away
from the angry crowd of ants,
They began crawling up the legs
of my pink cotton pants.

Brushing them off
I quickly took another direction,
Tis' when something so beautiful
caught my attention.

Looking up I could see,
colors of red and gold and green,
And all the colors of a rainbow
unlike anything I'd ever seen.

It's no wonder humming birds and butterflies
and busy bumblebees,
Were attracted to this special place,
full of breath taking beauty.

Today I had ventured out
in a fair garden of long ago,
Where lilies and daisies,
gladiolas and happy pansies grow.

Blue bells and cockle shells,
black-eyed Susan's, and hollyhocks,
Were surrounded by green ferns
and pink and purple phlox.

The many flowers on display,
overwhelmed the garden there,
But the most beautiful of them all
were the roses ever so rare.

One rose stood out amongst them all,
it's petals fully formed,
Its stem was long and slender,
its color of pink soft and warm.

The thorns had grown hardy enough,
to keep it safe each day,
From intruders who,
might try and pluck the rose away.

As sentimental tears fell,
I knew this rose could be no other,
Than the one who loved me first,
my dear loving Mother.

As a child I played in the garden
she so loved back then,
And for a moment in time
God took me there again.

Today she stands tall in His garden
so captivating and rare,
Surrounded by his love,
and one-day I know, I will meet her there.

Only The Willows Weep

The sun was shining
the rain had finally gone away,
Now it was okay for me
to run outside and play.

I ran down to the creek where
there were pollywog's galore,
And chipmunks and green frogs,
playing along the shore.

Lily pads were floating
with their lilies of white in full bloom,
While my bulldog Candy explored,
and would be barking soon.

Candy loved those little rabbits,
hiding in a thicket,
She tries to catch them,
but they are far too quick.

Butterflies of different colors
only found under a sapphire sky,
Would touch me now and then
as they fluttered by.

Growing in amongst the short grass,
were tiny purple violets,
Along with yellow dandelions,
creating a beautiful duet.

Birds perched in the branches
in the green lofty willow tree,
Sang in chorus their songs
which were carried away by a breeze.

Friendly old black crow
came scrounging now and then,
Searching for something shiny,
to hide in his nest again.

Robins were bobbing along,
selecting the finest of worms,
To bring to their little ones waiting,
in their nests so safe and warm.

Dragon flies were zooming around,
they never frightened me,
They wouldn't sew my eyes closed,
because it was just a fairytale story.

Lost in a dream land of my own,
was my happiest place in the world,
Safe from all the dangers lurking around,
for a very frightened little girl.

The sunshine made me warm all over
I hated for it to leave my sight,
For it meant I must go back in,
and then comes the night.

I preferred my safe place,
to hide from life's fatal blows,
Down by the creek,
beneath the weeping willows.

Only the willows weep
down by the creek,
When I'm there you'll not see a tear,
fall from my rosie cheeks.

Tis' my place where I won't cry,
Tis' where I'm able to laugh for a while,
Tis' where perpetrators aren't allowed,
Tis' where I'm able to forget and smile.

The Reflection I Want To See

When I look in the mirror,
the reflection I want to see,
Is your light Jesus,
shining each day through me.

Let your love flow through me,
in a generous way,
That I may pass on love,
to many others every day.

Guide my footsteps;
let my walk be your walk,
When I speak Lord,
let my talk be your talk.

When I greet others,
let your smile reflect through me,
Make me an example of,
what a child of God should be.

If by chance Lord,
I meet those who haven't met you,
Let your glory shine upon me,
that they'll desire to want you too.

I long to be your disciple,
until my day is done,
To be your servant everyday,
and rescue souls one by one.

When I look in the mirror,
the reflection I want to see.
Is your light Jesus,
shining everyday through me.

I Love You Daddy

When I was a little girl
I imagined having a dad,
A loveable but tough guy
to protect me from all that's bad.

I desired to feel special
in my somewhat painful world,
Have a knee to climb up on
and be daddy's little girl.

Swimming or visiting a zoo
would be fun doing it together,
Or sleigh rides down a hill
in the cold of winter.

Buying me a bike seemed interesting
and teaching me to ride,
Or father and daughter at the park
on the swings and slides.

I'd giggle if he pulled me in a wagon
and showed me off to all,
Smile if dad kissed my bruises
when I happened to fall.

I could listen to him
read me a story in bed,
Laugh when he tucks me in,
and tap me on the head.

Most of all I wanted a daddy
who would hold me tight,
When the nightmares frightened me
in the middle of the night.

I Needed a daddy
to love me in such a bad way,
Instead of having a dad
who turned me away.

God answered my prayers,
it broke His heart to see me cry,
And I accepted him as my Father,
as the years went by.

He loves me unconditionally
and hears me when I call,
And the greatest thing He taught me was,
How to forgive you most of all.
I love you Daddy...

My Silent Cries

Freshly fallen snow on the ground,
Crisp as the night air.
Muffled voices and laughter
Coming from
the living room out there.

On tender little toes
I tip toe down the hall,
Curiosity crowds my mind,
Has Santa come to call?

In pink flannel night gown
I venture out to see
Until I sense a presence,
Over shadowing me.

With fright I dare not move
I'm frozen in my tracks,
I feel a tug on my long blonde hair
I'm now ushered back.

Shoved into a room
Behind me shuts the door
In bewilderment I stare,
I've been here before.

Bad odor and appalling breath,
so sickening to me,
Makes me sick
inside my trembling tummy.

I cannot cry,
My tears are frozen in exile,
Long gone is
my inquisitive smile.

My tender heart is beating
Like a bird of prey caught in flight,
On this Christmas Eve,
in the cold dark night.

Screams can be heard,
but only in my mind,
Glaring at his figure
I want to run and hide.

I focus only on my silent cries,
Mommy...
Mommy...
Mommy...
Where are you
please Mommy.. HELP Me.
It's my brother Your son..
But no one comes.
And a small child's nightmares
have only just begun.

Flowers For Mommy

Dear Mommy:

When I think of you,
I picture flowers,
In a garden you so loved,
and tended to for hours.

I see you bent over picking weeds
with strategy and care,
So not to up root tiny plants,
tangled with them there.

Once in awhile you'd brush away a fly,
and then move along,
Humming all the while
one of your favorite songs.

I see your tanned face,
as you look up to blue colored skies,
Thanking God for the day,
while brushing the hair from your eyes.

As you busily dig with bare hands
getting dirt under your nails,
You'd toss away now and again
some rocks or slimy snails.

I giggled every time I saw you
chase our neighbors cat,
Your garden wasn't the place for him,
and you sure made him scat.

Sitting on the grass to rest a while,
you'd sip on your favorite soft drink,
Gazing at your colorful display of flowers
and taking a moment to think.

I often wondered what thoughts,
permeated your mind in your quiet place,
Because sometimes I'd see a frown,
then a smile appeared on your face.

Your smile mom, was it the pride you held,
for your garden so rare?
And the frown because of
a few flowers missing here and there?

Were you reminiscing on the times
when every once in a while,
I'd venture into your garden
and pick flowers to bring you a smile?

Were you remembering the way I looked
with tiny hands behind me,
Holding a bunch of drooped flowers
held ever so tightly?

Was your frown because I made you guess
what I had hidden behind there?
And was your smile the joy you felt when,
I handed them to you with care?

Were all those smiles for,
when I giggled with glee,
Because I received a thank you
along with kisses and hugs from mommy?

Was your smile and frown a mixture of
hearing my laughter,
And after I grew up,
could you hear me long after?

I do believe Mommy,
you held on to all of those precious memories,
And when you cared for that garden of yours,
I believe you thought of me.

Those flowers flourished,
and grew back from where I had taken a few,
But you never really minded at all,
because I picked them just for you.

Today you're in heaven's garden,
and there's no weeds to clear away,
Only breath taking flowers,
to make for a beautiful bouquet.

One day we'll meet again Mommy,
so keep growing those flowers so lovely to view,
Because when I get to heaven
I'll be picking some of them just for you.

Happy Mothers Day Mommy..I love you..

James M. Lowe II (negatvone)

Durham, North Carolina USA

My name is Jim. An ordinary name, huh? Not ordinary surroundings, I grew up all over the East Coast. Mostly Durham, NC. Electrician by trade, but poet at heart. I've found that this online family we all have grown to love known as The Poetry Pages has been one of the best places for me to release all the pent up feelings I've ever had. I'd still like to say it all wouldn't be possible if not for my family too. If not for my family in the real world; and my online family, I'd surely not be here this very day. This is for my family. I love you guys.

The Love Of A Mother

Destiny...... can it be this hard
Try to relive what's in your heart
The cannons fire without remorse on this bard
Freedom is left for an untimely depart

Sequenced shots from a firing squad shatter the silence

She walks on by, feeling into her soul
She walks alone

Love is in her heart
The past washed clean

Look into your heart
A message is left to be seen.

Blinded in the weaving of spoken lies
Voices cry for help to be shunned into the abyss
The will to live is sheltered; to fuel her unspoken cries
Tortured movements of thought still persist

Squandering hope she so readily tucked away
Reaching deeply into barren pockets for reprieve
Lost is her emotion; she's stuck for another day
Wandering hope still seeks her to believe

Everything seems so futile

Spare change found on the isolated bank of her soul
Simple pennies; a blessing so needed to ease the tension
Two cents to help fill a portion of this hole
Still, the loose change is gone without mention

Returning to the hole; in which her family now sits
She eases the famine with crumbs of her love
Still hungering for more than presented, the love still fits

Eager mouths consume the offering sent forth
The love of a mother can't be measured in worth

Even Death Leaves Me Behind

This brigade of thoughts intrudes into reality
What has happened? Why did this tear arise?
It was all sufficient, and then it went to purgatory
The mere shock brought the whole into surprise

My soul weeps for this closure, so dim and true
A thought of misleading all came to pass
My limbs grew heavy and mine thoughts misconstrue
Still, my heed I knew not to last

Attainments soon did contort to a withering decay
I was paralyzed from all movement, he was near
I knew this would all end on this very day
Deep inside my truth embraced this cheer

A solace so revered and waited upon
Blackening of the sight was upon my brow
The weight on my shoulders weighed a whole ton
This weight was changed to a lifting somehow

As I reflect I mourn on those in life
Souls raped as a commodity so easily dispensed
The pillage.. the hate... the strife
This torment was eased as this passing commenced

Then a breath, a scorned moment to be abhorred
Eyes open to another glimpse of light to be
Conformation was then in disgrace, detoured
For there was still life abandoned in me

A Sheep Amongst the Wolves

Compromise is just another contradiction
Set in your soul; a pouring of the waters sent ahead
In your heart this seeks the repetition
Contradiction leaves the want for dead

There's a place to be afraid and a chance to be portrayed

Look into your heart for the meaning that has been blinded
Shadows soak into the light of this offering

Unworldly desire set amongst the wolves to prey upon
Malicious and famished they devour my own words
Seeping want for hope does still creep on
Morsels of remains search for meaning of these blurs

Destiny strung high above; all I know is that you can realize

Scaring shadows of my past

Just another day left to the beckoning of a howl
A string of meat is the relish of my course
The wolves consuming into their bowel
This wicked surrender with none of its force

Wolves seek prey in dens

Home is where the enemy lies still
The field sought and again found empty
Hunting for the quench of the kill

A Dark Wing of Love

Desolately my heart contrives a moment of sanity
Reaching deep; I find a handle to grasp tight
Trying not to feel this prized calamity
I close my eyes and embrace the dark of night

When you're down you'll feel it

Just a melody of sharing stars
The breath of life like winding bars

Destiny can replace my wants in due time
For the moment I shiver in delight, so sublime

Your memory takes me over and over again
My love is for you; my one and only friend

Masses would gather to see your morning smile
A gift from above is what they would say
I've had you on the tip of my tongue for a while
Can I have you completely for just one day?

Pleasure is only measured when there is not enough to go around
The abundance of euphoria settles when you leave my side
Now I'm so exhausted I must lie on the ground

Bless me with your presence and allow the dissolution to spread
With a new day to abolish a memory of being; only to be read

Sunlight glistens on open peers
Left to view open eyes lent to tears
These wings of love caress me now
With this thought; I'll take flight somehow

Circles

Lost in patience demeaning my own reasoning
My mind so tired, still trying to expire from reality
Cooking the torment in like a delicate seasoning
Gazing in on the systematic consistency of the brutality

Silently waiting for a moment of reprieve

Inside an empty hole that closes and ends up suffocating
I talk with my self and find out that I'm not debating
I see that in time all will fall
For death will soon call

Screaming to myself; I see it all that all will fall
Barricades hold the sanity for the time now
In the darkness of silence, mental ears hear it all
The whispers of insanity's eternal vow

Another circle takes hold of the truth seen
This simple chance to wipe the slate clean
Heaven sends peace with you that tend to be the flame for me
It's all a circle that we tend to make for ourselves with this plea

Granted sanctuary on another rendition of the revolution
We will make it out of this step by step as our eyes are set
Grasping tightly on this ride; searching for the solution

Finding the frailty of my own structure as smooth
as the inner windings
Feeling the coarseness of the ride unfold
into blurs of comprehension
Loosening my grip on reality and all of its bindings
Keeping the gyration in desperately needed retention

Another pass in this ecliptic leaves me pondering again
With this new found sense of zen

Just Another Day

Just another day that passes by
One more melody to swarm my heart
Rhythmic streams engulf my sky
Hoping your love will never depart

Just another day

I'll never let this go
Grasping for the life I so desire

Just another day to share this sun
One more moment to hold you in my arms
With your absence my body lay in stun
Still, my body shudders in all your charms

Just another day to share the sky

Holding on so tightly, I grasp your light
I know that empty sands count on me
Sands of time that I so valiantly fight
Holding you forever is my destiny

When you are with me I feel so secure

Thoughts of your passing I must endure
Seeking your essence to fill this abyss
Drinking from your fountain so pure
In the end I must submit

Just another day to hold you close

A melody with pain left out
When you are gone I feel it
Angels sought you with a valiant scout
To keep me conscious, and in mind fit

Just another day you grace my presence
Longing for your lips to hold my captivity
Dripping sweat of your passions rain in its essence
Hoping my love is not perceived as serenity

Just another day we merge into one

Violent forces come crashing forth
Can we captivate this one more day?
For all it's worth

Broken Knees

I will crawl on broken knees
Just to be welcome in the gates
Drag me down to my elbows if that is what it needs

Don't lock me out

I'd crawl on broken knees
Just to find the light.
One more reason to fight

I'd crawl on broken knees
Just to take your hand and talk

I'd crawl on broken knees
Just because I know you'd make me walk

Ride the Lightning

Feel the emotion take the hold
Kissing winds so thrashing, bold
Telling stories in the days of old
Seeking the notion of sanity; bold

Nothing more than a whimper
Upon the flames we find the shimmer
A kiss of death that's of a thief
Emotions left ...... in misbelief

Sitting upon my throne at now
Wishing I knew just my query. How?
These nails have driven in my flesh
My soul has torment, no time for rest

Lay my head upon death's breath

Blow along in subtle course
Find the misery at the source

For everyone looks past me now
So close to rendering
But lost somehow

We meet in sight but I'm a ghost
To your vision.... A loss at most
No matter how many times we pass
Your vision on me.... Will never last

So, kiss the sky and tuck me in
And ride the lightning
Soul free from sin

Love, The Portrait That Should Be Painted

To break through a cloud is to be found within your sight

The sun hath no glory beyond your own shadow

Take my open mind and display it out for all to see;
For there is nothing beyond the reaches of you

A solitude grasps my own fiber that draws me close

To be blinded by the light is to be complete.
To be complete is to have my own desires broken

Just to be kissed by one more thought of you
is more than any man can take

Perfection treads harshly upon the weak of heart

Summon the Lords of War; for my heart can't take the absence

One more day of loss is enough to bring any man down.

Tread gently into my mind
Within my heart
You, there I'll find.

Withdrawl

My skin crawls
No matter how deep I scratch
Track marks left by my nails enthralls
Me to make another patch

Absence of life killing me within
False sense of hope to make it through

Feeling surrender with skin fire paved
Shaking profusely with madness displayed

Feeling like you must rip your own head off
To fight the urge
Nowing if it reoccurs; the deep end, you'll go off
Keep thinking purge

Sitting in a corner trying to abstain
Never wanting to live like that again
Hating yourself as well as others
Wishing you could fight with even your brothers

Nothing helps this madness
Drawn within a pit of sadness

Things that surround me all day
No longer; these things can I tolerate
This feeling appalls me

How many times will this change?
How long will I feel this strain?

My life is now over to make way for clarity.

Just A Word From Daddy

I thought you should know I love the way you pass
Just to hold you high and shelter your pain
Looking at the pictures of your youth and the limitless class
The endless memories cloud my mind like downpours of rain

My heart stops every time I gander at what you left me. The token
Tokens of love at first sight balance my mind on an instant
Even though you are so close, my heart is still broken
I just hope you deem my simple words to have subsistence

I never wished for anything more than you to find light
In every instance without giving up this simple fight
The fight was my own to duel within myself for you
Notice I have never stopped this unending duel and stayed true

I don't feel right when you have gone away
Not for a moment and not on this day
In my mind, we still go out for hours and play

Fields of green grass with us pummeling each other
Thoughts of you and your younger brother
My two children holding my hands covered in love
You two are truly my only gifts from above

Just remember how much daddy loves you till the day that I die
When this happens, I hope you never start to cry

Remember, love is eternal. I'll always be there

One Element

Find me within an element

Breathe me in
Hold your breath
for as long as you can

To miss one whisper of breath
Lost on fathoms of empty sea

Hold me close
I might miss one heart beat

Hear my words
Let them drip over open lobes

Feel my heart
I gave it to you

I am with you always
I will never slip away

Find us as one
Under open skies

Searching the same star
On our backs just one more night.

When the morning arises; kiss me softly
Let me know you have my breath

Look to the sunrise and know
This is why I'd give my life.

Prey

Grace my presence with one more day, My Love
Let's dance and sing and lie below the stars above
Hear the silence filled with your noise
Strumming gently upon my poise

Kiss the Heavens for this long needed moment
A constellation will be born just for us
Something to reprieve us of this torment
A quietness within this world's mistrust

Solemn moments that nothing exists
Not the bird, not the tree, not even the wrists
Not the wrists that one wants to destroy
Just harmony left to see; within this old ploy

I love you My Lady and nothing compares
Not the war in the world or the Ark with it's pairs

My life is yours to manipulate; it's your will
This strive for perfection still drives me inside
That one day you may see me in the same way; blind
Hoping not to be the victim on this kill

The Morning After

Looking on this window seal
Trying now; the pain must feel
Weary thought that has the light
To comfort heads upon this night

Seeking for the retention of the past
Knowing that the misery will last
Of hatred poured into my cup
Feeling mind's bends; awe struck

Kissing sheets seen as treason
Hoping now that there is reason
For the thought of this bliss
Fathoming times that my mind does miss

Stretching hope into the cloud
That this bliss lifts me to; somehow
Hoping that I'll never miss
The endless memories
This time of bliss

Kissing the sheets I wish you good day
Hoping in my mind.... One day you will stay.

Love at First Sight

I gaze into a thing of splendor
This one captive thing that my all must render
Losses of words as our eyes meet first time
All comprehension is lost; no sense of time

Twirling across the galaxy we go
Something more than my words can show
Imagery so profound and vividly seen
We glance into the lines and in-between

To see ourselves in what we need
Ravishing our tides in envy's greed
The taste of you is on my mind
Simple words are hard to find

Expressions of these twilight eyes
And the emotion comes as surprise
To the mind of me as we gently part
Silent to me it's in my heart

A Breeze

Watch the wind kiss flowing hair
Seeing innocence without a care
Just to have this day again
With this thought; left on end.

Dedicated to Gillian Chae Lowe. My precious daughter.
Daddy will always love you.
08/13/05

OriOnpheOnix

Michigan, USA

OriOnpheOnix seeks to manifest a spiritual/intellectual evolution through the shape of the letter. To further pursue his work, visit orionpheonix.com.

G2K

... Structurally abnormal or grotesquely deformed...

Self image seeps - Into the twilight of sight
Slow speeds - That are stealth
Arrays of eyes - Revolved by shadows
Kaleidoscope collisions - Incisions
In the slipstream - of the bloodstream
Complex corpuscles of a summer beam
Millions of hellion - Hollering vermillion
Outlets Inlets - For supernal platelets
Abolishing afflictions with healing agents
Harbored in hiding - In the monster blood

A portent sign - A monster design
A monster grid - A monster hybrid
A monster mind - A monster made
A monster staid - in A monster hood

Orbs pulsating flames - A monster stood
Absorbing the times - Oscillating street side
Grazing the sleeves - Scathing the selves
Scanning the hives - Scouring the lives
Implacably placing information in formation
Caravan of creatures - Masquerading as human
Comparable to a monster - Comparable to an alien
Cataclysmic caste - of a crash landing
Class classification - A classified standing

We fade into headphone zone - As we head home

Downward dangling

Ignite the candlesti x - Cast a spell
Watch me hover
Over
A full fledged absence of light

In these eyes
Is a shadow my daemon chose
In this place
of crescendos - Leading to lows
And sorrows

Sullied by tides which collide
Waves and whirlwinds we ride
A buoyancy of a hollow inside
Washed away
A shell on a shore
Sometimes a world is no more
Than ripples of downpour
That briefly shimmer
An infamous flicker
of a wish to explore
When it's all been seen before

A cyclic movement of closer and further

Upward dangling

A downward pirouette spirals to fragments...
Crystalline upheaval - Suspended digital
An epicenter center
Ripples and shrapnel - Crystalline petal
A shower flower
Conjured in a spatial - Space of reign of recoil
Each individual petal - Rises to celestial laments...

A fruition of sights seen - A colourless montage...
Opacity of a frozen - Figurative distillation
A severed tether
A trickle of a sickle - A rivulet to glean
A shatter scatter
On surface of a mental - Detrimental scene
A globule of people - Confined to a collage...

A godspeed constraint - A moment's levitation...
Chloroform scent sent - Into a stratosphere
A usurer mirror
Reflecting Quintessence - Cosmopolitan pure
A sheer vapour
Clamorous chrysalis - Reincarnation sure
Energy of essence - Enters evaporation...

A cyclical movement of closer and further

Sidereal dangling

Evolution of Evaporation
Colourless vapour - Baseless colour
Nebulous fleeting phantom - Emotionless base of spectrum
Ambiguous energy transformation - Nebulous mass godspeed
ascension

Into the SafireSkeyeS of a van Gogh starry night
Gaze down - On the town - From starry height
A station - of diamond vision - In starry sight

eye see... A disheveled Angel estranged by starry plight
A dividend of a divot - Delved into a wall stained by sweat
Below - A glistening glow - Shards possessed by pale moonlight
Smashed brash - Against a passed past - of absent minded regret

eye see... A felicitous Angel in a berth of starry delight
Focused on a future - As distinct as her allure - of velvet
A luminous luster - Maneuvers over illustrious hair - Forthright
Enigmatic factor - To see and savor left for another - To solve it

eye see... A sullen Angel unaware of her starry light
Under a vault of stars - She ponders - life love and the like
Aortic whirling tonight - A young man seizes her sight
Lovely appendages grip cigarette - Lovely - Never shall there be the like
On this rooftop divot - She is possessed by pale moon light
As SafireSkeyeS watch over ... HER ... Never shall there be the like

Ambiguous energy transmigration - Nebulous mass godspeed ascension
Nebulous fleeting phantom - Emotionless base of spectrum
Colourless vapour - Baseless colour
Evolution of Evolution

lower than the surface of this world of lines

ghosts invade the mind
a ceaseless sway
a foreign way
sublime
the way
time
travels away
in
tedium
in
spectrum
in
cerebellum
in
land of the broken ships

wasting away
in a day
which
slips
farther away
as every sun
comes with fresh tears
every destination
a return
from whence it began
a whole of a world
it ran in
a scan
of an
oval oblivion
caving in
only to return
breathing in
only to yearn
another turn
about it's axis
within
an access
modulation
ceaseless
foreign
entering a mind in sections of vivisection

a mind

lower than the surface of this world of lines

Vanishing ink

breeze speaks in dying breaths
hailed heroes dying deaths
unwept tears yield azure deserts
in the depths

dying eyes of sunshine
pallid precision
broken by branches reborn
somewhere in
reflection
in
black tints of a limo limbo
moving in
s l o w
motion
pixels of the picture show
motorcade of sorrow
moving in a chain of tomorrow

tomb stones stand solo
speak so low
"set the world on fire"
if I must go
I know
I don't wanna die with my eyes closed

BLA!

bird of prey
circles the cipher
remastered master
monolithic sky
chloroform form
molded from melancholy

as God dies
in our eyes

trees sway
leaves say

goodbyes

eye glide by... nasal sighs
reading the signs
venomous formulas as palate dries
blotched by blood whines
silken luxuries
of verbal vines twisting in brains

everlasting world without end remains
infected with heart worms
pervaded platforms
springing forth pollinated illusions

with withering conclusions
used to peruse divine dimensions
validating their see you agains
as fleurs
phonetically blooming in blossoms
from cores of cores
through holy holey lesions
in hamlet skulls
alone next to throne of safire souls
unimaginable flames
shifting spectrums

God is reminisced
in the mist
of an exquisite nothingness
BLA!

And we laugh

Green springs become blue.

An ethereal paintbrush fashions a period piece.

Seeking out perfection -
In an estranged abstraction.

Phantom birds in blue springs -
Tutor treasure hunted tears with songs.

Singing in a hidden place -
Through reborn downpour's shifting pace.

Slightly sullen sky sends -
Fragmentary prisms to slightly sullen lands.

Divined verdance displays enduring resilience.
Taking pleasure with one another.

Releasing burden in accordance to a musiQal cadence.
Mingling into the bleak background -

of phantom notes - Rings in rings ringing resonant.
Life's annulment absorbs into it's self.

Signature expanding in aloneness alone.
Defied by those who would defy death and self.

Adept at feeding death to fruition.

Resurrecting like pace shifts in mourning rain -
Which shifts and swirls in placental womb -
With razor blade sun - And wounded moon.
Womb like maggots fighting for position -
In the befallen plane of God's fallen brain -
Absorbing his own treasure hunted rain -

Flashes of his tenor and his domain -
Burst into a solidified floral flame -
To become his final perfection.

And we laugh

Jupiter Drops

my depth is equivalent - to the altitude
at which angels soar.

Without them – I am no more.

It was once tormenting to look to the sky.
Now I understand why.

Pacing through tombstone shadow.
On a path to the darkest meadow.

Sonar consciousness turns me into red and blue.

Fire and ice fighting with self.
In the incinerators of nightmares.

Blaze says – you have burned long enough.
Pain embodied in nothing really matters.

Send in porcelain into the nowheres overtheres.
Unfolding like eyeless stares

Where plasma waterfalls do as they were programmed to.

Bleeding selves in the manner we do.

Drainage complete – we are fire and ice – red and blue.

A broken walk is radiated by something healing.

Walk and see if you are followed by the feeling.

Plentiful surpluses to be carried away – are yours.

To be sifted and filtered into concealed and vaulted stores.

Cores of cores – treasured treasures – what you ares.

O... let us draw the shapes – to make todays of tomorrows.

CollideOscope

Apple invaded in a usurped displacement.
Emptiness promotes expansion.

Algae dark mold thirsts dosage of light to ignite - full blown fruition.
Barometric collapses leave molecules in stasis enmeshed with
dream of gestation.

CollideOscope suspension over wicks which wait to breath to believe
- in existence.
Precipice is – flames of darkness.

Eyes revolve in omnipotence of abyss.
Internal infernal.
Shedding blood letting like movement autumnal.
Falling fetal – gravitational granule – cross hair womb terrestrial.

Omnipotence of abyss revolves around formaldehyde fetus.

Memories are to be remembered in detached sorrow.
Crowned by epitaphs in a row.

apparition

faded reflections –
in dilapidated outdated
journals – journaling ascensions
and downfalls – bricks and walls.

all you ever were –
written shapes of sound
by her – alien appendage finger
in breaths the memories resound.

vapid to the taste –
of today – time has made
us this way – slowly yet posthaste
flames that have made and remade.

the monstAr before -
your very open arid eyes
perilous to the depths of your stare
configured in a colour of fallen skies.

a previous previous –
ink protected from a light
of a day – in drawer with key lost
like the rest lost to an eternal night.

secret of destruction –
is to be kept clutched tight
against your breast's construction
perfect in eyes that would see sight.

experience the shifts –
in chasms submitting scent
into senses which condense like sifts
taken for granted given to be misspent.

no man shall ever –
lie beside you in the manner
i did – never again shall your picture
be captured – like a captured summer.

beach expedient to our four eyes that were really one.

i told you i would exalt your memory and keep you on a pedestal.

EV(I)L(U)TION

Primordial ooze glows green – serene.
Blue mother of pearl – sends satin mantras in a swirl.

Supraface surface face of a moonbeam
Perfectly placed
Synthesis – into listless stillness of steam

Hand expands –
Into liquid window – from depths of nether lands.

Tombstone dome –
Breaks bond with sea – written in stone.

eyes slate grey skies –
membrane melting away to see – smiles and cries.

Chest caressed –
Life form forces form – up to waist of supposed waste.

Layers of airs –
Awakening of taste – beneath lairs of stars.

texture of pearl

out of the blink – the brink
of a dawn – from which we run

omnipresent radiation - of rays and fiery ways
batwings sing songs – of octane running
the gamut of sapped substance
sky fabric is a dividing soul

textured by hidden crystals
more lost than mad nomads of nothing
nothing - is the state of mind we find
deep in dictated diamante
penetrated by subtle shivers
which expose the synthetic colour of tears

we are artificial light and nothing more
just as we had always planned

all the impasses visited – a way we find
musical intricacies in the stones which follow us
as curved of the texture of a pearl

activate or reawaken the reactive centers
essence sweeps in chloroform form

emerald green crests of waves
as curved as the texture of a pearl

ecl*i*pse

Frozen in a poison position – admission.
Instilled with essence of enterprising moon over sun.

Eyes – skies... fires – mires... stars – fallen.
Into a spherical oblivion... painted in perfection.

Daggers float like fluid – through holes in souls.
All things implacably placed – into shapes and circles.

Swirling into cycles – circles and shapes – to be recycled.
Wicked world - circles shapes cycles swirled –
Painted platinum over base of fools gold.

Tap roots take root – in reservoirs –
Flood of blood – of - progenitors.
Fires – which blaze into theirs.
Neurogenentic predecessors.
Molten lava upon floors.

Rhythmic hallucinations.
Catalyst chemical reactions.
Attracted chemical attractions.
Illuminations in seas in fractions.
Ripples radar suspended animations.

Catalyst chemicals configured disfigured.
Fantasies flea into centers of sea – fractured –
Everything reality – partially impartially mastered – remastered.

Imagination a spiritual disaster which destroys – waits creates.
Etch marks in space alloy plates – etched out like dire straits.

Mad mad fates – nadir compensates – hallucinatory heights.
Mad mad flights – electric indigo nights – mad mad sights.

Sights gaits – partially impartially barbaric – archaic cryptic.
Elliptic liquid – seeping slow like blue nebulas shivering static.

Through a universe of verse – a haunted ghost on a haunted quest.

swirl@speed of sound

Seven swans upon -
White sails – engulfed by sun.

Hyperbolic staggers -
Pebbles stirred like stutters – and gleams.

Midnight noon - reverse moonbeams.

Voices come together - like water color.

Misty purple – swirl and circle.

Veins ventricle – swirling spell.
Swirl and circle – misty purple.

Pliant surfaced crucible –
Swirling spell – veins ventricle.

Mysterious mystique –
Material composition ionic.

Infused with more mystery.
An idea instilled with will – stains me.

Sustains me – restains me.

Serpent swallowing tail.

Sound of sea in shell.

everlasting eternal

godpaint drippings

Breeze and smoke create cold shivers on wings.
Color the texture – of godpaint drippings.

Drains consumed by the darkest shifting.

Relativity eclipses – eden with ellipses.
Pitches of plethoras – detonating visions in slashed eyes.

No light without shadow – no shadow without light.

Slashed skies – emoting in silent sighs.
Brush stroke breeze remains.

Shivering like wings.
godpaint drippings.

Somehow soothing.
Perfection in everything.

In between pulsating polarities.
Infusing clarities – into infused identities.

No height without depth – no depth without height.

Evoletah… queen and goddess of these ephemeral beauties.
Make masterpieces of these canvases.

Drains consumed by the darkest shifting.

Color the texture – of godpaint drippings.
Breeze and smoke create cold shiver on wings.

Terry McGhee (thief of dreams)

Seattle, Washington USA

Broken Pieces (Beautiful)

Young minds screaming release
Into bottles of blackness
Spiral down upon sands of safety
The ever elusive
Bedrock of beauty
Heartache shakes, cracks opened
Filling with the dust of time
Scars covered, poetry penned
Mister can you spare a dime?
Torn pieces of discarded blankets
Held tightly between clenched teeth
The scared and weary prophets
Spilling tears of madness underneath
Busy intersections, craving injections
Just a little something other than
The rejections and imperfections
We give them in our projections

Imagine

Soothing willow brook sound
Whisked away on winds of dreams
Comfort carefully found
Within streams
Polished perfectly while drowned
Superimpose visions of victories
Upon glassy water top surfaces
Reflecting life over trees
Haloed absence of preferences
Hidden within sinful deeds

Dark Leaf Poetry

forged in the flames of fury
plunged deep
into icy waters of retribution
the blade, the beauty
the perfect shine of sin
draped in the darkness of duty
waiting for the end to begin

Dark Leaf Poetry II

claws unravel past the shadows
sliding like liquid reflections
under the midnight rainbows
of dark recollections
the madness stirs to surface
within clouds of chaos
under a mind more abnormous
than terrors cast contagious
breathe to free the demons within
pray quickly for remission of sin
prepare the senses to beware
let the battle silently begin
quickly capturing the despair
of where we have been

Tear Away Today

Spin this dream away from me,
The barbed hooks covered in rust,
Sink deep and hold on,
My eyes betray my courage,
As I struggle in fear to tear away.
The stretch of skin,
The tearing of soul,
The ripping of flesh,
Until nothing is left.
Hanging and swaying,
Upon a hook of alone,
Beneath the tree of death,
Madness, bring it all home.
Innocent blood will drip from me,
As demons wait patiently,
Holding cupped claws ready to catch,
The last of my life, the ending plea.

Last Hope of The Lost

in life I see the dead
a dream, a fantasy
a lingering hope to know
that those I love
are still here
in subtle shifts of context
a cloud taking shape
a bird studying intently
a spider watching curiously
as I move through life
lost upon a path of time
a hand forgiving
reaches down to comfort

a voice of a stranger
filters after it
"They have gone to heaven."
I shrug out from under
the hand of isolation
look up to see shining eyes of happiness
fists curl silently
but my anger is not warranted
as I start to stand
whisper quietly
"Don't take from me the last thing I have.
Don't take from me, my hope."
I turn and walk away
feeling his eyes shift to sorrow
as his hands come together to pray

Regress Into Regret

the words still burn
holes within my heart,
knowing that I am the reason,
God damn my
Reason for being,
Breathing,
Take this air,
Disappear.
Some one slaughter me,
carve out this derelict heart,
and desecrate me.
Covered in cuts,
Drowning in tears,
convulsing upon the floor,
I can't reach the door,
In time,
To answer,
A knock.

Fucked up and obliterated,
Everything I ever
Reiterated.
Damn me something fierce,
Bandage me in blistered flesh,
I'm holding the stake,
All you have to do is push to pierce.

Releasing Peace

Razor blades
Of wretched relief
A drop of blood
To fill a belief
Such chaos reins
Inside the mind
Swirling down drains
Of what we hope to find
Belief
Believe
Someone please
Believe in me
Voice echoing off empty walls
A shuddering breath let loose
The screams that shatter crystal balls
The want for acceptance outside a noose
The trails of blood that line the halls
An angel lies draining away
Wishing only someone would say
I love you
Please stay
I need you
Please don't fade
I am proud of you
It's going to be okay

Double Spaced

A little star winks down
Smiling cheerfully at me
Explodes without a sound
The dream
That keeps failing me
Tendrils of terror
Coarse through my veins
The shadow bearer
Of terrible things
Fists clenched in forgiveness
I pray for a dreamless sleep
But the nightmare persists
In fear they will keep
Relentless
Torment buried deep
Release me
Please
God
?

Awe Struck

Stumble into the new
Sunshine blinding, unlocking
The midnight binding
Heartache blocking
Walls of wish full
Sanctuary
Freed to breathe once again
Even though she knows
Of where I have been
Her laughter still flows
Captivating me in comfort
Fueling the fury in which love grows

Finding Fortune

Shutter free of shelter and find your wings
Love can lighten the darkest of things
When by your side a goddess resides
You can roll back the oceans tides
And bask in the warmth a woman brings
Feeling like the jester that defeated the kings
While welding a welcome that closes divides
And embracing a future the promise provides

...

Dropped down through the fogs of alone
Stumbling upon the wet cobblestone
I fall into your arms as phantoms dance
Spiraling up into a new romance
Sealed with a breath before the first kiss
Bubbling into a romantic bliss
And time slows to a crawl
As my arms secure a hold
On beauty before the fall
As your fingers remove the cold
From my heart and dance to scrawl
A love worth more than gold
And together we will conquer all
Lifted up by loves embrace
Staring at an angels face
Holding tight to the welcomed release
She soothes the fear of the inner beast
Gives me courage to carry on
I'll hold her forever past the last new dawn

Dedications

Sands of time slip away
Spiraling through the cyclone of time
Ocean currents move and sway
Shifting sands unable to climb
Into towers for too long
Before tides rise past a lifetime
And take us back to where we belong
Emotional tides ever changing
Mourning a year of time passed
Five lifetimes of exchanging
Tears and laughter unsurpassed
Midnight mourning
Mixed with crying smiles
Lifetimes of remembrance
Scribbling of trials
Of an enlightened darkness
Through uncountable miles
Of homelessness
Into a world of awakening
Captured in smiles
Between Bar Wars and Flashback
You found a balance
A foothold in the crack
That I will remember in your absence
With tears upon a smile
Until you come back

Miss you Jenn

Dealing With a Pedophile
** warning: mature content and language*

part one~

Alone and scared
A dark night, a damp alley
Sitting with my back against a wall
My only blanket pulled up to my chin
Trying to stay awake
I can sleep during the day
Watch as men and women walk, stagger and laugh
Their way to the next bar or club
A car drives by the end of the alley slowly
I pray its not a cop
It passes without incident
I turn back to watching the people walk by
No one sees me, yet they walk right by me
But that's ok cause when they do see me all they do
Is throw a beer can at me or laugh and pretend
That I'm a drug addict or a fool
But I'm not
I'm just a kid, fifteen years old
A young man with nothing
Only two shirts, one pair of pants
The mud covered shoes I wear and my blanket
I didn't have any time to pack a bag
I didn't have any time to say goodbye
But a kind old man from the streets
Gave me an extra shirt and this blanket
He was very old. Only fifty one
But on the streets that is very old
A wise man, who lost his life
His wife and kids
Everything.
Who shared with me a few things
Advice only, but priceless advice it was
But now I sit here watching the people

And another car slowly rolls by
Familiar
It's the same car
As before
But now its turning into the alley
Shuts off its lights and rolls on
Coming closer
I fear this more than police
I've heard of things, people who
Hurt people like me
Even kill if they want to
If they feel like it
I gather my blanket and stand up
Ready to run
The car stops a few yards from me
A silhouette of a man gets out
Stands by his door and asks if everything is ok
"yes sir, I'm fine."
He asks if I need money
"no sir, thank you I'm fine."
'but son' he says, 'you look like you could use some extra money.'
Please go away I think to myself
But I say,
"well if you have any to spare?"
a question
a soft laugh, 'nothing to spare son.'
Then, 'but I could pay you for your help'
"my help?" I ask
his shadow nods, 'here, come here and have a sit son.
My car has a heater. Warm up a little and we'll talk.'
My head is screaming NOOOO!!
But my feet shuffle forward
'that's good son, here have a seat.'
He reaches over and opens the passenger side door
Click, the over head light comes on
He curses and reaches up to shut it off
I stand, not sure what to do
'here son have a seat.'
He pats the seat beside him

part two~

'here son, have a seat'
he pats the seat next to him
my legs are shaking with fear
I don't want him to see that I'm scared
I climb inside, the heater is blowing hot air
It feels good, warm. Familiar.
'what's your name?' he asks
so I tell him and he nods
doesn't offer his, and I don't ask
I'm pretty sure I know what's coming next
he rests his hand on my thigh
'so tell me,' he says 'what are you doing out here?'
"I ran away from home."
'oh I see' he says and slides his hand up slightly
I wonder if he has a gun or a knife
No way of knowing. I don't want to find out
I pretend I don't notice his hand
'have you ever been with a man?'
"no." barely a whisper
'ever thought about it?'
"no." I glance down quickly at his hand
he slides it further up. Touches me
I should have kept my blanket in my lap
But I put it on the floor at my feet
A million thoughts run through my head
Should I run?
Should I scream?
Should I hit him?
Knock his hand away?
Let him keep touching me?
Can anyone see us?
Will the cops come?
Money? He mentioned money
How much would I get?
A hundred dollars?
More?
Ok, ok. I can do this

He just wants to touch me right?
I hear a zipper
Oh my god, he unzipped his pants
I pass a quick view to check
His prick is in his hands, hard.
'do you think I have a big dick?'
no! no! no! no! this is wrong!
"I don't know."
His right hand is squeezing my crotch
It hurts but I'm too scared to say anything
'do you want the money now?'
"I uh. I don't know."
Bad choice of words. Damn.
'I'll pay you good, if you touch it.'
Don't do this. Please don't do this.
What was I thinking? How stupid of me
Fucking idiot
Fuck!
He reaches over and takes hold of my wrist
Pulls it over to his prick and puts my hand on it
I don't really try to pull away
I'm too scared
His prick is hot, hard. He moans
'oh yes. Mm. Pump it.'
he won't let go of my wrist,
squeezing harder. So I do what he wants
'mm oh yea son that's it.'
he tilts back his head, and he starts breathing hard
then whips his head up and looks at me
I cant see his eyes, its too dark
I know that if I could id be even more scared
'want to suck it?'
"no, I better go."
'oh no you little tease.
I want you to suck it.'
Then before I know what's going on he grabs me by my hair
pulls me over the center console
pushes my face onto his prick.
'suck it.'

oh my god why me?
Tears well up in my eyes, I just want to cry
But I hold back the sobs
'suck my dick son.
Remember I'm paying you for this.'
He twists my hair in his hands
Pushes my head down further
His prick is hot against my cheek
Then there's a blast of bright light behind my eyes
He hit me, oh god the pain
My ear is ringing
I just want to go home
Please god, do something
'suck it!'
so I do.
With tears in my eyes
I suck his prick
I can't think of what I'm doing.
I just do it
Then something hits the back of my throat
I start to gag.
Oh my god
I know what it is. Oh god no
'swallow it.'
no I can't. Please
he hits me again and I cry out
cum falling from my mouth
he hits me a couple more times
then he shoves me away
I rake my fingernails trying to find
The door handle
There, I got it
I start to open the door and he pushes me out
'little cock sucker!'
I hit the ground and lay there
He reaches over me to grab the door
Spits at me and slams the door then backs away in his car
I lay there crying
No one sees me

Where is every body?
Sobs burst from me
I lay racked with sobs. Tears streaming down my face
My left ear is still ringing
I can feel my face starting to puff out
I look up towards the end of the alley
And realize he took my blanket.

Jenni Meggers (Phoenix J. Star)

Arkansas, USA

I am a mother of one child, now 2 years old and I work for the Visitor's Bureau. I have been writing for 11 years and I feel that my knowledge only grows and my writing abilities get a little better with age. No matter what anyone says, my writing is mine and I love it.

An Argument with Myself

Where did the confidence go?
It's still there...
back and forth,
coming and going...
Why is this so important?
Why do I care what I look like?
Growing up in a tight knit
family...they tell you everything.
Every pound you pack on...
every blemish on your face...
every imperfection you implicate.
Because YOU are not perfect,
YOU will never be perfect...

That's why you do it...
that's why you only eat barely
one meal a day...
perfection.

You are no longer perfect...
you never were.
Why can't you realize that?
I do realize that...
that's why I have to
lose weight...have perfect hair...
have those shoes...that purse...

You're not in high school anymore...
why do you care?
I never stopped caring...I can't help it...
Every time I start to love myself,
here you come to remind me that I'm not
perfect...go to hell...
already been there...
well go back!
I can't until you're perfect again...

I guess you'll be waiting a while...
Take those diet pills,
they'll help you lose weight...
Having a baby helped you gain
a couple pounds...

I was pregnant!
I was supposed to get big!

You're not pregnant now...
SHUT UP!
GO AWAY!
Don't make me do it!
I'll do it I WILL!

You'll do what?
Go fish for compliments?
Go ahead...

BANG! CRASH!

Oh god, what have you done?

Coffee Stain

Coffee stain, go away.
Leave me be, let me
stay sane.
Words of pain, are all
you know, hurtful tears
from long ago.
You drive me crazy,
to the point of
sober drunkenness,
Coffee stain, leave
me be.

And She Cried...

Once a strong woman,
she now feels weak,
having to let go of something
so familiar, something
she'd known the majority of
her adult life
but she did
and she cried.

Her home and family
ripped apart, most of the kids
gone, a couple still at home,
coping each in their own way,
moving forward from day to day,
but she still cried.

Why so sudden?
How did she fail...
or did she fail at all?
Was it just people growing
older, but not growing
together?
She did not know,
and she still cried.

Tired of the pain,
tired of hurting every day,
she let him go.
With her family by her side,
to love her and help
guide her new life,
when she goes to sleep at night,
she doesn't cry
for him
anymore.

The essence of a weird memory

The memory is a bit foggy,
seeing as the occurrence
was many years ago,
so the details are a bit
scattered, but I remember
a small portion.
I was about 8;
we were vacationing
in Eureka Springs,
staying at a Days Inn.
Gran and Ninny were inside the room
unpacking and I was right
outside the door
playing with something…
don't remember what though.
Then I remember looking up
from sitting on the concrete
and seeing a Goldwing trike.
I didn't know what in the hell a
Goldwing trike was when I was
8 but the guy waxing it
was going on and on about it.
He was probably in his 50's,
almost 60's.
I had always been told not to
talk to strangers, so I didn't.
I just sat there on the ground and
played as this old guy rambled on.
He asked me if I wanted to look at the
bike, I told him no thank you.
He said, "Well I won't hurt ya"
I again said no thank you.
He asked me if I wanted a ride,
I said no thank you.
He then walked over to where I was,
bent over, and told me he would take

me to get ice cream.
Once again, I kept my
Head down and said no thank you.
Next I remember my grandmother
Opening the door,
and yanking me inside.
From there I'm sure
she asked me what he said
and I'm sure I told her,
and that was that, but I
often look back and wonder,
what if I would have been one
of those nice little girls who
thought "OOH Ice cream!"
and jumped on his Goldwing trike
with this complete stranger?
Would he have taken me
to some remote
part of the woods and do
God knows what to me
and leave me for dead?
It's scary to look back at
that...but I can't help
and wonder what
would have happened?
Would I even be here today?
Who the hell knows...?

And She Came Home

After being away on a
binge of selfishness and
false euphoria...
she came home.

After giving up all
the things that really
mattered for some

fake friends and
a hit here and there...
she came home.

After hitting the rock
bottom of the well
only to realize what
life is all about,
realize what she wants,
and it's not this life...
she came home.

She came home tired;
she came home sick,
probably a bit delusional,
head still probably a bit thick.
But she's home now,
in safe hands,
she knows she's alive,
she knows where she stands.

The little boy that was
constantly in the back
of her mind helped
to bring her back to Earth.
The family that loves her so dear
makes sure she knows that they
all are there, through thick and
through thin, they're there...

and she came home.

A Willy Wonka Kind of World

At some point in our
long but short lives,
we must all come to grips
with the fact that we are
no longer babies, children,
teenagers, young adults,
middle-aged,
and that one-day we will
in fact be "elderly" and
probably senile, slowly
scooting around with our walkers
talking to walls, and things
and people that aren't there.
But on this prolonged yet
quickened journey through life,
lets not dwell on the fact that
we will be old one day.
Let's enjoy the time we are given,
the people we are blessed to share
this time with,
and the many triumphs and
tribulations we must endure
although try to avoid.
Rome wasn't built in a day,
and the sun will probably
rise tomorrow.
What's the use in feeling
sorry for ourselves because
we don't have fields of candy
to frolic through,
and everlasting gobstoppers
don't really last forever.
We will probably never have
some nice man who owns a huge
corporation gives us a golden ticket
to the easy life.

There's just no way around it,
and there's no use in crying
over spilt milk...

It's Not Only Rock n' Roll

*BOOM! BOOM!
CRASH! CRASH!*
Beat after beat I can
do nothing but listen intently.
Watch his movements, his facial
expressions as he beats those
drums senseless.
His arms flailing all about,
knees bobbing up and down beating
that bass drum,
hair dripping with sweat,
watch the fire in his eyes.
A fire lit with a passion,
a passion for music, a passion
for this heavenly yet thunderous
instrument of percussion, drums.
Drums, symbols, crash and ride.
High hat, bass, snare, and tom.
So many combinations played,
yet many to be combined.
With the collaboration of guitars,
acoustic, electric or bass,
magic is born, music is made.
Music is born in him.
When inspiration fills his
brain to maximum capacity,
he must release it into
a series of beats.
Release his fury
into his music.
Play.

Operation Freedom

As children walk on their way
to school you can hear bombs
exploding in the background,
terrorizing their homes, families,
tearing apart their very existence.
As they walk to what they hope is
left of their schoolhouse already
in shambles from years of war,
they will try to concentrate on their
studies, although their thoughts drift
away to their families at home,
will they have a home to go to
or will it be just another pile of rubble?
Meanwhile there is fighting in the streets,
suicide bombers around every corner,
to take the innocent lives of more
women and children in the name
of their Allah or Saddam Hussein.
Soldiers stand around, some standing
still, some on patrol, some wondering why
they're there, some positive of why
they're there...to give these people
something they have never had...
freedom...
Freedom to speak freely,
freedom to live freely,
freedom to fight against oppression
with being oppressed.
Freedom to uphold a democracy
instead of tyranny,
Freedom to be people who have their
own opinions,
Freedom to simply be free...

Abbi Jean

Your not here yet, but how
beautiful you will be.
Either hair of gold or
of dark like the night.
Eyes of blue diamonds that
sparkle in the sun, and a
smile that will melt
millions.
Will you play the piano
like your mother did
for years on end, or
will you be a drummer
like daddy's dream?
Will you play guitar,
or dance with God's grace?
Will you be a tomboy
or a gymnast so agile and
flexible?
Will she be a writer
who touches others with her
words of grace?
What ever your destiny may be,
Whatever path you choose,
know from now until forever,
you will always be my Abbey Jean.

Double Jeopardy

Things happen to you sometimes
that you just really can't believe
happened at all.
that's when you have to sit
back and evaluate the situation,
and do what you have to do.
But sometimes these situations
that occur hit you very close
to home and you find yourself having
to make a serious decision against
someone very close to you.
You have discovered that forgiveness is
really not an option right now and you
are so beside yourself with these
difficult choices you know you have
to make.
You make your decisions totally based on
your own well being and what is right
and wrong only to be condemned and hassled
by your own blood.
What do you do now?
You don't want people mad at you,
yet you want to do the right thing.
Decisions, decisions.
You know what?
Why are you listening to them in the first
place? You do what you think is best.
do what is right.
Spare no feelings. If your feelings
weren't spared in the midst of this
act taking place, then there is no
reason for you to be the nice one.
Stand up for yourself. If your family
won't back you up, you know your
friends sure as hell will.
Look inside yourself and

find that strong person who isn't
going to put up with stuff like this.
You are in no condition to take it
just as the culprit was in no condition
to make the stupid choice he made.
The deal is done.
There is no going back.
It's out of your hands now.
You did what was right.

Boredom

So here I sit at my desk,
watching the hands on the
clock move slowly backwards,
forwards a smidge, OH, then
backwards again.
The people around me seem to
be moving in fast motion as I
dwell here wondering why my
perception of time if so different.
Everyone has tons to accomplish
before the clock strikes five,
and myself sitting here as if
I have a mouth full of sand.
As the day drags on, at a slower pace
than it started, I remember I have
been here in this same situation
before.
This is boredom.

You Know? It's Not That Bad

Life is full of drama,
that a given fact.
When life hands you those
drama lemons, just take em
and stick em up who ever's
ass is making your life hell.
Cause you know? It's not that bad.

When the grass on your lawn is
looking brown, and dead,
just look at your neighbor's
yard full of dirt, and be happy
you at least have some grass left.
Cause you know? It's not that bad.

When you get yourself all worked
up over small things, remember
that someone out there has way
worse problems than you do, so
stop your cryin and get over it!
Cause you know? It's not that bad.

When you wake up and the sun is
shining, and you still want to
shoot those damn birds chirping
outside your window, at least
do it with a smile on your face,
cause you know? It's not that bad.

When you feel that you have no
one who wants to hear you whine
about your problems, or the person
you are whining to pretends to
care but really doesn't, its probably
because they have problems too, just as
everyone on this miserable planet does.

So don't get mad at them and
seek out revenge, ask them how they are,
and if they want to talk about their
problems, cause you know?
They might be worse than yours,
and life is too short to waste your
valuable oxygen complaining.
That oxygen might not be
there in 10 more years and if you
actually stop to think about it,
life isn't that bad.

Lobotomy

I'm walking around aimlessly
inside my brain, looking for
the muse, to end the strain.
It's dark and lonely up here,
so empty and gray.
I'm left here wondering,
How long will it stay away.
So much is happening
in my life today.
But still nothing comes my way.
The words used to flow like
water down a stream.
Now it's frozen, as if covered
in moss of green.
How can I be a great writer, if
no words come to mind.
I suppose I'll sit here and wait,
till the next time...

Hiding Behind the Mask

When you see me walk by,
I look completely normal
and happy to you.
But don't let looks
deceive you,
inside this bubbly
blue-eyed girl,
there is much anger,
resentment, and pain.
There is a soul that has
been walked over
time and time again.
There is a girl who
has worked hard for nothing,
wanting nothing in return
other than a simple
"Thank you".
I try to ignore the pain,
but when you're all alone,
it's hard to concentrate on
anything else.
I try to look at the brighter
side of life,
I tell people all the time
that things aren't as bad
as they seem,
and tomorrow will be a better day,
when I don't even practice what
I preach.
I have patiently been waiting
for that day when I wake up
in the morning and get excited
about the day that lies ahead,
and I'm still waiting.
When I drive home everyday,
I'm not excited that I'm there

because there is somewhere else
I'd rather be.
Where?
I don't know, anywhere but
here.
I don't get excited to see
you because I know you have
better things to do rather
than spend time with me.
I make an attempt to
tell you how I feel since you
think that I keep my feelings
from you,
but would you want to talk
to someone who only puts you
down for the way they feel
even when you are making them
feel that way?
I feel as if I have no choice
but to hide my feelings behind
a mask,
since everyone only wants to
see the mask, and not the real
thing.
I don't think that I'm
sitting around feeling
sorry for myself,
I don't have time,
all I have time to do is
put all the worries,
frustrations, fears, and pity
behind this mask,
so that I can be me to all of you,
and move on with life as it is,
and keep on keepin on with a
positive attitude,
but always knowing that I don't mean it.

Once a Child

Once a child, now a mother.
Life has a new meaning
now that it all has begun.
Children's laughter and smiles
mean much more than they ever
have before.
Once a child, now a father.
Life has gone down an
unexpected turn.
Time to grow up, but there
will still be time to play.
Once a child, now a mother.
Worries that have never
crossed her mind, fill her
everyday thoughts.
"Will I be a good mother?
Will I do everything right?"
Once a child, now a father.
Stress of a different level
begins to sink in.
Dizzy from the thoughts,
"Will I be able to provide,
Will I be a good father?"
Once they were children...

Ninian

Winnipeg, Manitoba Canada

I started writing poetry and fiction as a child. In recent years I founded an internet poetry community, which included a poetry chat, an e-journal and several poetry conferences. I won the Writer's Circle award at the University of Winnipeg in both 1984 and 2004 and though I dabble in other genres, I write mainly romantic poetry.

Your Words

Your words, chosen precisely
to convey exactly what you mean,
captivate me.

In an effort to keep touching them,
I overcompensate --
for the silence hangs comfortably
between us.

Toxic Shock

I sit,
as I always do,
  when forced
to talk to you,
coiled and tense
like a spring
  under pressure.
I listen vaguely
  as you whine
about your work
and its
    toxic environment.
    Funny.
For you have breathed
your poison
into my lungs
  for years.

Cognac On Coral

It was the summer of our memories.
The hot southern sun kissed my skin to golden brown -
the colour of lightly toasted bread .

I wore a floral sarong
and coral lipstick.
You pampered me
painting my nails a corresponding shade
washing my hair in rain water.

And in the evenings;
You taught me to crack crabs,
to swirl and sip cognac;
and hold it briefly,
warm on my tongue.

In Other Words

Your words spoke to me
So I gave you some of mine
And the chain continued.
Every moment another link was added
With neither of us hearing
The subtext in the language.
          (cautious review, no editing allowed;
                    something we both do constantly);
And tentative connections revealed.
The love of words,
compared, explored, and quickly shared.
I dance as Barrett with your Browning
Our love of words
Giving us each other.

Running Between the Raindrops

"A picnic in the woods" you said
So we packed the blanket
and a basket with wine and cheese and fragrant bread -
just baked.

You held my hand as we raced for the shelter.
"Hurry, we can go between the raindrops"
Pulling me to you
damp under the tin roof,
you kissed me hard
licking the rain off my lips.

I hung suspended in the moment;
shivering slightly,
my light cotton dress wet and clinging to my legs.

You wrapped me in the blanket,
watching the fire you started,
and opened the wine.

The flames flickered,
like lovers in a dance,
the cheese and bread were left in the basket
forgotten.

sinryu

morning arouses
as you rise to greet my lips
and comes the new day

The Middle Of Trust

I have an image of you and me
on a hot afternoon
sitting somewhere --
in the middle of trust --
eating fruit.

The juice dripping down my chin
laughter bubbling up,
as you lean in to sticky kiss it away.

I want you with every breath.
You are my first thought on waking
my last on going to sleep.

You encompass my world,
without ruling it --
speak to my soul,
without uttering a sound.

You know what I want before I voice it
what I need before I need it
where I am before I get there.

And who I am
is always me,
always with you,
in the middle of trust.

Untitled

Come to me in silence
with touches that reach
soul deep.
We have no need of words.

'Til Niagara Falls

And then, the summer that we met –
the heady rush of your smile
your warmth surrounding me.
It was a summer for falls,
white noise waters blocking out everything but
the sound of my heart beating.
You, attentive to my need, as I
pitched headlong over the edge without the barrel.
There, like the waiting water,
your arms outstretched
to catch me.

Shared Silences

let me walk with you
in the greening of spring

to the secret place

where we are
twinned souls

connected
without connecting

communicating
through silence

together
even though apart

parallax

i'm pulled
by ellipses into
your silences, filling blanks
with words you couldn't say.
I turned at the connection to
that place I wasn't going, left breathless,
in the middle of trusting you. And, living
in this world of them, we have no need
of words – drawn to the same point on the map –
and if I look carefully, I'll see you were always here.

Strawberries

I bought strawberries at the grocery store.

They conjured up an image of you
from that summer long ago.

You fed me strawberries ripe
and warm from the sunshine.
You laughed as I polished my nails
a matching red.

Your eyes crinkled up into a smile
as you held each piece of fruit
just out of the reach of my lips.

Even now, the taste of strawberries
makes me smile.

The Colour Of Your Passion

I want to write for you,
twisting images into words,
the way I tangle the sheets
when you fill my dreams;
but the muse escapes me.

I want to sing for you,
blending harmonies in celebration,
the way the nightingale
serenades his mate;
but the notes evade me.

I want to paint for you,
mixing the ambers, blues and greens,
an impressionist view
of our love;
but the brush falls from my grasp.

I want to bloom for you,
glowing in the first blush
as a spring rose, baby pink
its heart a deep red;
but too soon the petals wilt.

Instead,
I wait for you.
When comes the time,
I will write, sing, paint, bloom,
always for you.

Inhaling Your Essence

The mellow sweetness of you
after making love.

I trace circles in
the droplets
round your navel.

I smile secretly
watching you sleep

    eyes closed,
       lashes
          brushing flushed cheeks

      mouthopen
        quietdeepbreath

Kissing your forehead,
I curl up beside you

holding our warmth.

The Art of Syncopation

My timing was always off --
And I am continually amazed
at how you can dance
to my syncopated beat
with no faltered steps.

Lost In You

Our eyes met and
the connection was obvious
to those who cared to notice.

A faltered step, but then
you smiled, in your easy way,
and it was like flipping a switch
inside my heart.

And if, when we hugged,
my feather-soft fingertips
brushed the back of your neck,
I don't think anyone noticed.

And if my body,
feeling at home in your arms,
lingered overlong,
I'm sure that no one saw.

But, you noticed.
And you saw.
And you smiled.

The Cost of Time

Come, spend the summer.
Blue and gold days,
trading shiny copper pennies for sweets and sours
languid in the midday heat.
The teasing sun
playing hide-and-seek behind the clouds.
Rainbows arcing from the crystal sprinkler
icy cold on our golden brown skin.
Fingers sticky from popsicles and watermelon
Or sugar dipped rhubarb.

The world was a different place
seen through the heat distortion over the sidewalk.
Endless days of bikes and roller skates
Iridescent bubbles catching a passing breeze
or snapping thick dark ones in the tar on the street.
Inevitable thunderstorms brought rain turning to hail
giggling under our garbage can lids collecting stones
big as golf balls.
The days wound down to August,
the summer spent, our pockets emptied,
the smell of new paper, rubber erasers and pencil shavings
getting us ready for the new year of school.

The days, it seems, no longer stretch endlessly
from June to September, the gap is bridged in the wink of an eye.
No time now for running through the sprinkler or blowing bubbles,
tar makes no sound when it is driven over.
Spring skips to winter so fast I hardly notice
And popsicles get messy when they melt.

But,
You said those magic words;
"Come spend the summer",
and time stood still.

In the Moment

I'll speak to you the words of love;
Stolen kisses in summer's rain,
Silences and fingertips,
Pleasures shared once again.

The moments we will share, my love;
Wine and candlelight,
The softness lit by fire's glow,
Passions in the night

When We Were Dancing

Take my hand
and dance with me,
while the band plays
all our favourite songs
from the golden days.

With the rise of the moon,
the flames flicker high,
we whirl around on the polished floor,
our hands held tight, arms outstretched
spinning, spinning
to each thump
        thump
        thump
of the bass drum.

We'll do the Lindy
and jive ourselves around –
a flick of the wrist
and we're doing the twist,
then sliding into a samba.

As the night grows long,
the fire burns its way to coals;
we sway beneath the stars
arms clasped, chest to breast
our hips slowly swaying
to each beat
        beat
        beat
of our hearts.

The Promise of Spring

A breath of spring air,
your voice whispering in my ear,
fans the spark in my heart
to a flame that takes my breath away.

Rainbow-coloured dreams
caress my soul through your words,
feeding the flame that consumes me;
our bond so tight, I can barely breathe.

The Promise Broken

I long to go with you to the spring place
where we were both young, and in love.
Where reality held no limits.
But the feeling changed,
I never thought you could let go
                and mean it.

A momentary fantasy,
left me so turned around
I barely recognized myself --
        a lonely soul rubbed raw
        a shattered ego
                and me --
picking up the pieces of my reality
finding that coincidence is really only that,
and connections can be found anywhere
if you know how to look.

Puzzle Pieces

We fit together
the smooth curve of back to chest
leg to leg
hand to breast.

You blanket me as I slumber
placing kiss-caresses on my neck and shoulder,
my personal guardian
keeping nightmares at bay.

The gentle nudging of you
pulls me early from dreamland.

The feather touch of your fingertips
chases away the darkness,
raises shivers over my skin
down my spine
and warmth spreads from within me.

Dancing On The Edge

The dance we do
has no choreography
but we both know the steps.

Careful to skirt the edges
of the stage – we dance on –
as mirror images.

Each of us incomplete, yet
unable to give in, and complete
the other.

We take only the steps
which we have set for ourselves,
afraid to try new ones.

Staying in the light
though the pools of darkness beckon, enticingly,
we avoid them,
dancing at their very edge.

In dreams we meet and dance the steps
that in daylight we avoid.
In dreams we celebrate
our dance of joy.

More Than Friend

I sit and breathe the fragrant flowers here
While knowing that the snows are coming soon.
My heart is longing for your presence, dear,
But might as well be longing for the moon.

A second summer's come and gone for us
Another winter holds me captive still.
And we're still sitting in the midst of trust
Together in our hearts by force of will.

So, I sit and scribe you poems by the score,
As if mere words could cause you to appear,
Each line I write expresses my needs more
Your presence still is feeling rather near.

     My love sings out for you in lines I've penned
     The depth of feeling so much more than friend.

Fighting The Drown

At a time when I needed a life preserver
you threw me an anchor.

The weight of it pulled me down
sowed the seeds of my self-destruction
crumbled the facade of my perfect life
and a thousand other clichés.

Tearing my world apart piece by piece
drove me to the brink of reality.

I've drifted back in my foggy haze
to something resembling my normal life
but it is haunted daily by the ghost of you.

Faltered Steps

Did we lose the way?
Feet once so sure,
falter now on the path.

The climb seems so much harder
without the constant reassurance
of your hand holding mine.

And I know the steps I must take
must be taken alone.
But they are harder, now
that I can't see
your footsteps
ahead of me.

2:00 AM

the ache at night
in darkness when i hear
the quiet rhythmic sounds
of your breathing
        but you're not there
and the memory
        brings me back to reality
         with a thud

"I'll never leave
        (oh but you did)
"I'll love you always"
        (but only from a distance)
"I respect you too much"
     (but not enough not to leave me
       broken
         shattered
          vulnerable to the ridicule
           of those wiser in the way
           the world is
          who tell me I'm too good for you
        I can do better
      You don't deserve me)

my bitter tears
make me angry

        even without contact
        you have this much control
          over me

Dennis Schmunk (Eternum 1)

Christina Lake, British Columbia Canada

I currently operate a resort which allows me time to write and share poetry with the wonderful people at Poetry Pages. I am passionate about poetry and the people I love. I hope these words bring you, dear reader, a measure of the joy I felt while writing them.

She Writes Poetry

As she writes poems
of erotic seduction

That fill the silent
corners of my mind

My image of her is unfocused
a haze of soft gossamer in lacy black

Her bare footprints through wet paint
trace the desires in my mind

A slight whisper of indulgence
teases the skin covering these words

My whispers follow hers
like Masqued courtiers at Versailles...

My poem is the fingers in the breeze lifting your dress,
the phantom touch teasing your nipples.

My poem is the pillow that opens your thighs
as you sleep curled like smoke around a dream.

My poem is the touch that causes dew to trickle
between your thighs as you open your legs to pleasure.

Neither bed nor meadow will hear
of this seduction so discreet.

For I am the lover of her otherness
her wantonness and her words caress

As she writes poems
of erotic seduction

Another Okanagan Summer

Another Okanagan
summer gone
leaves curl golden
in pages of
autumn's hymnal,
the scent
of spiced cider
clings from uneaten apples
as vines dry to husks
on the pickets,
shadows stretch
and beckon the end
of this summer,
this place, almost abandoned
except for insects, drunk
on the fermented echoes
of summer laughter,
unheeding the mystery
of death and rebirth
written in frost, each morning.
I will forget
this time
this place,
summer's canvas,
now stored
in the gallery
of my belonging.

Whisper Me Home

You whisper my name,
as if it was smoke
rising from the heat of your passion

I whisper yours to Mons Venus
with wet kisses
stirring amongst lotus petals

Kite ribbons of hair drift across me
in sensual counterpoint to rowing hips
pulling us towards the waterfall

I forget who I am
as all star charts fail me
like cat's eyes blinking

Now lost in vermillion waves
scarlet sensations,
our hands speak a language of their own

They speak in roaming braille
to the hidden crevices
and peaks of us

Embracing, awakening
'til you whisper my name
and whisper me
home

Love's Measure

what is the measure
of love lost

the threshold between
memory and regret

loss is a word for amputees
regret is a word for cripples

one is a measure of love
one is a measure of fear

I vow to embrace love
with complete abandon

I vow to abandon
regret

I will love you again
in the heart's genesis

when tales of love in books
are written in the shade of promise

you will read my strange words
feel them and know

that mortal life is too precious for regret
and love is never lost

Smiling Buddha Lips (Country Lyric)

Standing on your rain swept porch
is a wind blown meadow lark
Like a piece of jigsaw puzzle
in a pic of Noah's ark

Just another bit of magic
with no remote control
I just found the program
that looks into my soul

You know I love you darlin
show me what you feel
Maybe a slice of heaven
in the cards that you deal

You got the power lady
to read my astral stars
Should I head down the highway
a pilgrim in the bars

I need some soul guidance
to get me on my knees
We could do a séance
where granny shoots the breeze

Maybe I'm just crazy
because I believe in you
I'd put you in my sticker book
like a page at Sunday School

You cant say I have no faith
because I believe in you
You could be my savior
my palm line says its true

Give me some religion
set up the fiery hoop
Let me sign on the dotted line
for your transcendental group

You could be my idol
with those smiling Buddha lips
I could walk on water
                those hips

wine
thy self
time

heal
ach other
eal

within

religion
with a side of halo rings
and a choir of busboys tapping time
while Lenny Cohen sings

Come be my cathedral
invite me inside
I'm standing outside in the rain
forget your foolish pride

A Solar System For Two (Acrostic)

E *ach time I read*
R *omantic messages*
O *nly she can phrase*
T *ension stirs my body and*
I *see her as quintessential woman*
C *aptured in tantalizing haze*

P *oetry revolving in slow*
O *rbit like the moon pulling tides*
E *mulating gravity in sensual movements*
T *hat tease me, just enough to*
E *nvelop me with tangible desire,*
S *haring her erotic dreams in a*
S *olar system for two.*

Summerland

lay with me on soft earth
dust your skin
beneath dappled light
in the hollow
of rowed grapes
red and ripe for tasting.

taste my lips
on yours
savor the cup of us
while grapes
fall from the vine
perfect in their vintage.

Lady and Blue (Lyric Ballad)

I took Blue out walking
the Pacific Coast range
With flyrod and flint-box
we're traveling companions
Blue chased down a rabbit
to sauté with onions
We agree on everything
and that doesn't change

As the moon rises
we sit by the fire,
blink at the starlight
and curious deer
Blue has my promise
one day I'll retire,
Stay in our mountains
where the air is so pure

We both like the ladies
as much as the moonlight
Blue makes no promises
and he don't drink a beer
I once wed a woman
to cherish through the twilight
Blue wore a collar
and a sharp button'eer

The Lady and Blue
shared my life's highway
The Lady and Blue
saw all to see
'Til I get called
to our home in the skyway
The Lady and Blue's
all I need

There's a prayer
men whisper
when sailing
rough weather
There's a prayer
men whisper
when death
comes along

A prayer of thanks
for every bright morning
A prayer of thanks
for sending Blue along
A prayer of thanks
for the Lady who loved me
A prayer of thanks
for sending her my song

** Inspired by Tom Watson and dedicated to him with gratitude.*

She Writes Poetry III

in my home
by christina lake
where i await,
nestled among
evergreen hills
and snowy blankets

anticipating
the swell of her breasts
the scent of her womanhood
to melt away
my heart's frost

as i read her poetry
she becomes the mosaic
of textured memory
softly supple
in my strong hands,
like eden's clay
i mould her

would i recall the perfume
of her inky phrases
on folded paper
in the worn pockets
of my coat
as i embrace her
at the door

no words
as my lips brush
hers and warm
hearth fires glow
because she
writes poetry
and poetry
brought her

to my home
by christina lake
where i await
nestled among
evergreen hills
and snowy blankets

Summer Storm

A whisper of silkworms
as your kimono falls to the floor

Orchid petals color
as night becomes you

Quickening my sex
thickening your desire

Quiet enchantment as
you encircle me with your lips

A moth beats against the shutters
as I brush my lips against your thighs

Summer thunder counts miles away
as my tongue slips inside you

Mouth to sex we recite
the symphony before crescendo

Intermezzo as I lift you
like Atlas to rock my world

The freshening wind opens the shutters
and cools the sweat between our bodies

In bold ménage-à-trois, the storm's
breath envelops us with its passion

Our entwined limbs
vibrate to it's electric desire

I glimpse you riding me
with wanton abandon

Light fills the room
as you shudder in completion

Answering thunder
masks our sounds of pleasure

Soon, soft rain falls
through the open portal

As the scent of moist earth
joins our musky wetness

Like the passing storm
now, content to sleep

and leave the night
in peace

The Man In The Moon

you look at me
as you walk by the sea

your lover holding your hand

i've been inside you
your body, your mind, your soul

i've been with you every night
since you let your feelings show

the glow of my sexuality
radiates your skin, invites love within

my desire is endless, it is timeless
for you are my desire made flesh

mortal lovers are waxing candles
thrusting, dripping and disappearing

i am the first trickle of heat
between your nubile thighs

the ache in your breast
for a loving caress

the peak of your orgasm,
the tantra of teasing

the spark in the gloom
with lips the most pleasing

i am the man in the moon
above your earthly perfume

and you look at me
as you walk by the sea

your lover holding your hand.

Silence of the Spheres

I gaze upon the heavens
The silence of the spheres
Hints of the last pure celestial note
The moment after crescendo
When the conductor exits the stage
To walk in the garden of his creation

God Made Woman

As a pair of thieves
we disrobe
to enter a secret pool
as quietly as leaves

Did Eve look like you,
sending waves of desire
rippling through water
like twin flames afire?

I see my sex floating
in the water
With an intuition
and some bother

That God made woman
despite our belief
Then made man
for comic relief

Writing My Goodbye (lyric)

I watch the boatmen rowing
through the mists of Avalon
While blackbirds were crowing
over a fallen fawn

That's when I knew for certain
it was my time for leaving
Your bedroom with blue curtain
and the widow's gown you're weaving

The raven is my brother
and the robin is my shame
I was your season lover
and the seasons always change

I'd linger for the moment,
until I loved my fill
Your charms are so potent
I might stay here still

I know my soul is craven
I know it's not my place
To sing 'aint misbehavin'
and wipe your tear stained face

My love, you are married
and now you're feeling guilty
It's been too long I've tarried
enamored by your beauty

I'll see you in the river,
I'll see you in the morning,
I'll see your face forever,
wherever, I'm exploring

I missed you by a fraction
when wedding bells were tolling
You've been the main attraction
since women I've been knowing

I'm writing my goodbye
with a fallen ravens quill
If you look unto the sky,
it reads.....I love you still.

Song for Chloe

If I was real tiny
I'd rope a bumble bee
Nestled in its soft fur
ride over the flowery sea

If I was gigantic
I'd hold my arms up high
and catch the other planets
as they went flying by

I guess when God made me
he thought of other charms
It seems I'm made just right
to hold you in my arms

at this point Chloe giggles and says your funny granpa

Beyond Words

He writes poetry
like a traveler
to a foreign country
She writes poetry
like a castaway
far from home

Both write poetry
like acolytes
in candle lit cells,
surprised by words
ascending from depths
to kiss each mind
with symbiotic ripples

Is there a world
where their thoughts echo
off canyons,
where sound is a color,
A dimension opened
for their twin souls sanctum?

Thought is the path
that brings them here
Emptiness, the path
that leads them home

Do they intuit
the language of rain,
Of soil and sun
in paper under pen?
As they write their song
in harmonic symphony.

Will they awaken to the voice
of this world
To forget
their music
Now echoing
in the other.

Paper is made
from rain and sun
Seeded by the wind

Poetry is made
from souls yearning
Seeded by whispers
of the heart.

Perhaps they
will see through
this veil of being
while the canyons hush

and a muse
takes them both by the hand
to the new world
they are making
beyond paper,
beyond words.

Sunset On The Sea Of Cortez

Color of red lips
on turquoise sea
tints Spanish villas
into pink vanillas

Through crested
palms
Sols parting kiss
touches a sea
of diamonds

Mango scented breezes
waft through balconies
as lovers
open their blinds

Widows in black lace
chuckle
in remembrance
of sensual siestas

I sketch your nudity
in charcoal
as an offering
to the Incan Sun

Autumn In Christina Lake

Pewter grey clouds fill the sky,
And the paths are strewn with the red and gold of nature's confetti.

Dry nesting places break under foot, and the barren willow, sways and
droops as perching ravens herald winters call.

Mulled odors glide aloft on wings of sun's waning beam,
bringing scents of deep wet barrows and brown appled decay.

Canada geese trumpet resplendent in christina lake,
and waddle like fat dwarves on the shoreline.

Behind, the woods watch mute and await the murmur of falling snow.

Cones drop from pines like the challenge of gentlemen's gloves,
As a lordly elk tosses his crown of velvet,
And the doom of wolf's eye is lit with golden gleam.

Silent trout burrow deep in a stream, their silvery light in murk, unseen.

Look now! The pilgrim geese rise up from their bed,
with flashing wings and sparkle of dew,
taking to autumn's sky, sulking sullen over-head,
forming an arrow-head, pulled
straight from my soul.

I remain, wounded, yet wishing
them joyful sojourn
and safe
return
home.

Lamarr Smith (foreverflame)

Columbia, Missouri USA

I am 27 years old, living in Columbia, Missouri and since I can remember I have always been a writer, whether it was a story or poem, childish or serious. I always enjoyed the freedom in writing...being able to stretch my imagination. I take interest in other hobbies, but writing by far has always been my favorite.

That mysterious masterpiece of miracles

...Paintbrush...
...still and idle
until flesh grabs it
and instills a mind to it.
Giving it motion that scripts a dream
that is seen as a 3-D pictured scene.
...Now life...
...courses through all its makings
that appears as all sorts of assorted paintings.
Inanimate object made so still...
...until the hands of a mind came and gave it will.

...Piano...
...ceased and stopped
until flesh makes
its keys unlock.
Giving it melody that shakes the strings
from a mentality that shaped a dream.
...Now life...
...flows through ears that listen
and hear the sounds the mind has written.
Soulless creation froze in placement...
...until a mind comes and activates it.

...Paper...
...bare and empty
until flesh comes
and shares its thinking.
Giving it thoughts dispersed as text
that creates a lot of diverse effects.
...Now life...
...brims through words and flow
from what one's mind has learned and known.
Lifeless material made simplistic...
...until a mind makes it into an invention.

Colorshade

Black trees...
...underneath a charcoal sky.
Hear the whistle of the gray-shaded wind blow by.
Black sun...
...standing over dark black streams.
See them blend in the night, no reflection seen.
There's me...
...staring...
...on the grass I lay.
Shaded in an array of blacks and grays.
Gray cloud...
...parts and start to divide
as a ray emanates, darting down from the sky...

Then a color beautifies. Blue and white return to skies.
Streams again flow crisp and clean as grass and trees return to
green.
Sun regains its fire shine as winds return to sightless fly.
Once again upon the stream the sun's reflection can be seen.
I look and start to smile wide...
...it seems that color's back to stay,
until I look down and I sigh...
...for I'm still shaded black and gray.

Gray flowers...
...growing from the pitch black dirt.
Smell the gift of scentless scent they give to the earth.
Black stars...
...pasted on the dark night sky.
See them sending off a vision of invisible shine.
There's me...
...staring...
...in a captured gaze.
Shaded in an array of blacks and grays.

Then the ground...
...parts and starts to divide
as a ray emanates with a colorful shine...

Then the flowers that are planted get a colorful enhancement
as the air regains its fragrance from the flowers that have made it.
All the dirt upon the ground becomes enriched with colored
browns.
Stars are dotted through the night sky, spotted once again with
white shine.
I look and start to smile wide...
...it seems that color's back to stay,
until I look down and I sigh...
...for I'm still shaded black and gray.

Why oh ray do you forsake me?
...hide me from your colored glow?
Why must I remain in shade
with colored dreams I'll never know?

You are dressed in many colors,
but of them you are ashamed.
It is you who tries to hide yourself
in shaded blacks and grays.
Beauty takes its place upon you,
but it's something you don't see.
So instead of "colorful"...
...you see yourself as "color-free".

In a bottle

If life was in a bottle,
would you drink it sip by sip?
Slowly trying to taste the good times,
while the painful times you spit?
Would you take it and reject it,
and just dump it on the ground?
Never knowing what its taste is...
...its adventure never found?
Would you put it on the shelf
and face it's taste another day?
Putting off your want for it,
for fear of what may come your way?
Or would you down it in one gulp?
Take it in for what it is.
Leave your worrying behind you,
so you have some room to live.

Reversible Swordplay

Blade to face, his eyes chase it's shining.
On the ground he lays, his own blade lays behind him.
It re-drags the ground till it re-found his hand.
Leaps back to his feet...rebounds back in stance.
Blood backpedals back from the handle as he holds it.
The strike to his hand is pulled back by his opponent.
He thrusts out backwards as it's counter-blocked high.
His opponent stands, spinning sword counter-clockwise.
His heart beats wild, as he hopes to find an opening.
His opponent smiles, staying deeply trenched in focusing.
He says to himself "...hard be will strike One"
as his opponent says "Garde En! student me strike, Come!"

Reversible Nature

I tread backwards...
...through the fallen leaves
that have fallen from a tree in the autumn breeze.
I look at the tree, then crack a grin
and say *"you seen I've since while a Been."*
A leaf that had fallen atop my hair,
reverses and floats back up in the air
connecting itself so it's stuck on a limb,
then changing direction as it's sucked by the wind.
I keep back treading 'till I fade in the distance.
Some leaves on the ground start to get uplifted.
Slowly they rise and grab on branches
defying their ties with gravity's enchantment.
One by one they float and sail
back to the very branch where they broke and fell.
Once connected, they remain on the tree
and change from brown to a shade of green.
There they sit as time rewinds
and makes the branches reduce in size.
The leaves turn to buds as the branches shrink
and the tree doesn't budge as it starts to sink.
Closer and closer it gets to the earth
as if someone is pulling it from under the dirt.
Smaller it shrinks and little it gets
until its trunk is the size of a stick.
Time flies by 'till the remnants of the tree
are inside the confinement of a little bitty seed.
There in the dirt, the seed resides...
...until a young, curly-headed boy comes by.
He waves, then says *"grown I'm when you See!"*
Then he falls to the ground and digs up the seed.
With his eyes closed, he speaks his mind
saying, *"grow you Hope. here you plant gonna I'm."*

Parallel Dictionary

Friendship: two persons with trusting faith
Enemy: two persons bonded in hate
Love: emotion. Unexplainable joy
Hate: anger. Emotional void
Understanding: to know what it is you speak of
Judgment: comes when one is lacking the above
Pity: compassion. Sometimes leads to "giving"
Envy: despitefulness. Gives "tunnel vision"
Compliment: a gesture that strengthens belief
Degrade: a gesture that puts one beneath
Acceptance: comes when one treats other as self
Rejection: when one treats other as something else
Sadness: a peak of depression. Makes "tears"
Joyful: an upbeat expression. Makes "tears"
Smile: expression of face. Contagious
Frown: a down-look impression on faces
Confidence: when one stands out strong without help
Insecurity: when one's not so sure of one's self
Courage: fortitude. Keeps one forward facing
Fear: anxiety. Makes one lust for safety
Death: stopped animation of movement. Produces "fear"
Life: animation mixed with all listed here

Mind findings

I sift through corners and borders...
...hoarding geological finds
lost in psychological minds...

...fossilized...

...I find that each line describes
an era where a thought was made,
but tossed aside.
Reasons why are inconclusive
and not constructed.
It seems these minds were more elusive
then they were productive.

Excavating the soil
from a spoiled invention
that shows traces and hints
of great intent,

...but...

Left to rot
in an uncharted spot?
So unlikely a mind
would hide such a thought
of important release
of mentalogical peace.
An immense start
that ended in resentment and ceased.

Pulling junk out of the ocean
from the depths of mentality
and finding a gathering
of sensational imagining.
Wipe the dirt and grit
and spitshine the fixture,

then sit and try to figure out
the depths of its splendor...

...mystery...

Again, an inconvenient incompletion
of a though of great proportion,
yet aborted and deleted...
...but I see...
markings all across its core
Seems these findings have seen
some part of war...

...unexplainable...

Findings of astonishing make,
yet highly degraded and thrown away?

Perhaps they were rejected
to form some defenses
against those that won't accept
an "intellectual existence?"

...Hmmm...

Perhaps their craftsmanship and build
foretold a tragedy
of being pushed distant
from the status quo of "reality?"

...Hmmm...

Or maybe they were detested
as a form of aggressive evasion
from a disgraced acceptance?

...Hmmm...

These psychological finds...

...with a make so exalted,
yet halted...
...and lost from time...

Let me fly away tonight

Let my worn heart shine tonight...
Please, let my torn heart fly tonight.
Let pain not pour out hurt no more,
Just let me soar through skies tonight...

Just take me...
Far from those that hate me.
Free me...
Leave me to my dreaming.
Love me...
Let the winds come hug me.
Hide me...
Let their eyes not find me.

Take me so high
in the sky...
Let breeze hit my eyes
as I fly...
Wings I will not need
I will rise...
Just let me be free
in the skies...

Let my worn heart shine tonight...
Please, let my torn heart fly tonight.
Let pain not breathe its hurt on me,
Just set me free in skies tonight...

Unbind me...
Let my mind go flying.

Hold me...
Warm me from the cold freeze.
Lift me...
So I'm with the winds' breeze.
Keep me...
So I'll always be free.

Take me from here
Let me flee...
Let pain not come near
Let me breathe...
Wings I will need not
Let me be...
Just let me take off
Set me free...

Let my worn heart shine tonight...
Please, let my torn heart fly tonight.
Let pain not try to hurt my mind,
Just let me fly away tonight...

Through the hurt

Punch me, hit me, bump me, kick me,
Stab me, hurt me, grab me, curse me,
Cut me, scratch me, judge me, slap me,
Hate me, down me, break me, pound me,
Poke me, strike me, choke me, fight me,
Beat me, tear me, bleed me, scare me.
Bring your worst, then still your eyes...
For through the hurt...I still will rise...

Metamorphosis

...metamorphosis...

The boy is playing with Tonka trucks.
Down on his hands and knees making noises (honks and stuff)
Then he sees a bird with a broken wing, so he goes and picks it up
and starts to gain a deep compassion for animals that have it
rough...
...and has a...

...metamorphosis...

He grows up and becomes a vet,
but his compassion slowly passes due to huge amounts of stress.
People blaming him and framing him for things he can't correct,
so he gains hate and chooses not to wait on others and their mess...
...then comes a...

...metamorphosis...

His hate grows deeply dark in time.
Losing care for life...whether his or theirs...and deep in drugs and
crime,
until the judge slams down his hammer, yelling "You'll do 5 to 9!"
Then he thinks, "This can't be me..." as he's escorted out in binds...
...he gains a...

...metamorphosis...

Now he's in prison, where he waits.
Sometimes crying, sometimes trying to cope with life by lifting
weights,
until he spots a bird outside that's hurt, he tends its wounds, then
thinks...
"When I get out, I'm going to be a vet. I know now that's my fate..."
...then comes a...

...metamorphosis...

We're always going, always growing
from what life is always throwing,
we're remaining ever changing...
...due to our...

...metamorphosis...

The static of silence

In silence I am weightless,
shapeless and faceless.
Incased in the basics
of the nothing that makes it.
I am foolproof from fools who
could fool you into
doing whatever the hell it is
that fools do.
I am unharmed and equipped
with unarmed equipment
disarming your alarm
that you get when you "listen".
I'm the glitch in your data
of systematic propaganda
turning your repetitiveness
into irrelevance.

In silence...

I am a ghost that roams
with rest, yet still blessed
with flesh and bones.
I am preserved
through unheard words
that would unearth nerves

that give birth to slurs.
I am credited
with an unedited trance.
Putting eyes in debt
from their inept glance.
I am findless from minds
that try to find signs
to tie into a lie
and pry into my life.

In silence...

I am given a home
that is blessed
with the gift of being left alone...

The touch of dust

...All that I touch...
Every person I meet
when I'm out on the street
when I shake their hand-
...It turns into dust...
-it cracks and it breaks
from their feet to their face
then they turn into sand.
...There's nothing but dust...
Every time there's a hug
it is empty of love
so the people all change-
...When there's nothing to love...
-into pillars of dirt
that are scattered and hurled
as they're all blown away.
...All that I touch...

Every smile I see
lacks the care that it needs
so the people just crackle-
...It turns into dust...
-and break into sand
in the place where they stand.
Not knowing what happened.
...There's nothing but dust...
Every laugh from their mouth
has some dust that comes out
because they really don't care-
...When there's nothing to love...
-since emotions are lost
in the void, and the cost
is that nothing is there.
...All that I touch...
I see my reflection
is cracked at each section
I feel the dust come-
...It turns into dust...
-as it pours from my cuts
I think "So, this is what
happens when there's no love..."

...it all becomes dust...

Visibly cloaked

One is visible...
...only through a multitude of mysteries
that forms their present form
through the honing of their histories...
...a list of things...
One's been through, gone through, fought for, seen and done...
yet a glance at first will not by chance
unearth a single one...
...for they've become...
A figure cloaked in writings
that most eyes have hard times finding.
Being seen, but sighted not...
...Though eyes do see, they're finding naught.
Behind the scenes their depths do thrive
and strive to show their meaning to eyes
so those who see their cloaked disguise
will understand it's written signs...
But alas...
...their past is key to present
that frees the meaning within their presence.
Bought from time and stocked in mind,
but locked inside...
...too hard to find...
So on they go...
...with great descriptions
coded in cloaked encrypted depictions.
Constantly knowing
that what don't show
will just be something
that some won't know...

W.J. Thomas (chthon)

Kingston upon Hull, East Yorkshire England

I live in Yorkshire, England where I am the proud father of a wonderful daughter. I started writing poetry (and prose) in my early teens, but work demands and family life meant that for many years my pen was stilled. I recently returned to writing and found a home on 'the poetry pages'. Though most of my work is dark in nature, thankfully few of them are autobiographical.

Daddy is Here

I stood, bewitched by your tiny beauty,
my world forever changed.
Your little fingers clasped my heart
and I embraced the newness of you.

I told you then I would always love you.
Be there for you.
Would pick you up when you fall.
But you fell too soon.

As the monitor beeped
with its mountains and troughs,
I watched as its landscape
diminished.

Through the darkness that enveloped
my world, your light broke through.
So small, yet so large in my life.
As years pass, you remain clasped to my heart.

Daddy is here.
If only you were here too.

When You Were Three

You came to me with mouth down-turned
And asked why you
Did not have a Mummy
Like all the other girls and boys.

I sat you on my knee.
Explained the reasons why.
You cried for you,
And so did I.

We hugged and dried each others tears
Then you looked at me and asked
'Will you be my Mummy, Daddy?'
I had to look away, to gain control,
lest I started weeping again.

'I'll try my best, my darling',
Was all that I could muster.
And you smiled the smile
of innocents.

Then you asked, 'Could I have an ice cream?'.
I knew Mummy would have said 'No',
As it was nearly dinner time,
But Daddy said 'Yes'.

Behind the Door

I cower, frightened, behind the door
hearing noises I've heard before.
The daily battle of shouts and screams
(embittered voices lace my dreams).

My only solace, to shield my ears
and hide away from all my fears.
As parents quarrel in loveless rage
I squat forgotten at five years of age.

Until the violent words of hate
abruptly stop I sit and wait.
Not wishing to be alive or dead
I close the door and go to bed

Alone, with teddy my only friend,
I cry to sleep and await the end.

A portrait of me

My head is large and orange.
Arms from ears emerge.
No body. Just spindle legs
from my chin.
Eyes black and misshapen
adorned by sunburst lashes
compliment my off-centre nose.
A mouth of smiling teeth
framed with red-cheek blobs.

I have no hair.

I do not recognize
the portrait.
Though it must be me
as it is entitled 'My Daddy'.

And it is beautiful.

Soulmate and Lover

Sometimes
I see your face
and hear your laugh
and wait expectantly
for the electric-tingle
of your touch.
Though I do not know
who you are
or if we shall ever
meet.

Fighting Spirit

Breathing.
I am a dead soldier.
Resigned
to my fate.

Leg and belly
bullet-punctured
leaking life.

Trusty comrades
death-masked; despoiled.
Trusty rifles
ever by their sides.

Drowsy wind-whispers
drilled with fly-buzz
breathe wet-wounds
through hazy-space.

Potential threat! Telescopic-site survey.
Swept vista. Contact made.
Identify. Mother...Infant
Categorise. Red-wet...Crying.

Assessment. Life.
It's cold at night
but darkness and ice
are mud-footed nemeses.

Lazy afternoon
pregnant with pain
and the wailing
of a dying child

remains.
Blazing sun.

No victuals but sulfurous air.
Feral dogs and feral men -
potential acquaintances.

Pink phlegm
lung-bubbles
in ripped-flesh
spasms.

Conclusion. Damage limitation.

Twice shocked air
resolves *to silence.*

Suffer the Little Children

the children lie quiet
they make not a sound
their faces angelic
with innocence found

the voice in my ear
tells me to prepare
a lamb for the slaughter
so i say a prayer

i carefully sharpen
the ritual knife
ensuring it's keen
for the taking of life

so peaceful my children!
and peace will be yours
forever and ever
Amen, says the Lord

The Cave of the Dead

There's a man in a cave with a candle for light
as the storm rages on in the dark, torrid night
He holds his own counsel as he writes down his fears
and the pages he's written are sodden with tears

He weeps for the many for the ones Man destroyed
as the death-rattle surges in the doom-ridden void
He's alone with his thoughts on his last day on earth
alone has he been since the day of his birth

He's loved and he's lost and he's loved yet again
but because he is Man there is nothing but pain
Theres no one to love him and nobody to love
so he raises his eyes to the darkness above

And with his last breath (just a faint, gentle sigh)
he asks just one question - the question is 'why ?'
Now the papers are scattered, forever unread
and the candle's extinguished in the cave of the dead

Harvest

I harvest your kisses
and reap your love
storing my desire
until next we meet

Counting My Tears

The
Thwup!
Thwup!
Thwup!
of leather on leather.

Tenderizing
my flesh to a healthy
glow.

Brothers and Sisters
look on with taut
canvas smiles as I
am punished
for their wrongdoings.

I am five years old
and
my mother is wielding
the strap
and
my siblings are counting
my tears.

I am alone
with my silent
screams.

Happy Thoughts

The lisp you had at two-years old
the bubbles from your nose
spaghetti sieved through fingers
and mud upon your clothes

The way you laughed when tickled
the evenings at the fair
the way it took 'forever'
to put ribbons in your hair

The mornings when you'd wake up
and climb in bed with me
and make me pretend breakfast
with pretend toast and tea

The nights we read together
before you went to bed
the times you said 'I'll do it'
then did something else instead

The parties on your birthday
the tears when you fell
the secrets that you shared with me
(though I promised not to tell)

The days out at the seaside
building castles in the sand
the way you called me 'Daddy'
and the way you held my hand

These things I oft remember
with a smile upon my face
as I place some fresh-cut flowers
on your final resting place

Sorry

The door is closed.
I sit in silence
with ruddy cheeks
and runny nose.

And hug myself
expectant-waiting
listening for the footsteps
that will surely come.

Only the faint
silver sliver from the door
encroaches in the cupboard
beneath the stairs.

I fear of naughty beetles
and squirmy things
that lurk unseen
but brush my skin.

Eyes wide
I try to see
shadows moving
through musty darkness.

The skin beneath my eyes
is tight where brine
has left its invisible etchings
as it dried.

I will be rescued soon.
Mummy will take me back
into the light
and love me there.

And I must say 'Sorry'
and promise
not to be bad again.
Until the next time.

One Evening

I heard
the wailing first.
The screaming.
The curses spat at the wind,
drawing my eyes to the tenement doorway.

Police. Ambulance.
Blue lights reflecting from grimy windows.

A sheet draped in one man's arms,
small contours beneath,
halted my breath.

All I could hear
for the rest
of the evening
was the voice of a tortured mother
screaming 'My Baby! My Baby!'.

In the morning,
walking by the same building,
all was quiet.

Deathly quiet.

That Was Then

She said, 'I'll see you later'
And I replied 'OK'
As she closed the door behind her
On that fateful, final day.

Just a few hours later
The 'phone began to ring
So I picked up the receiver
And my world came crashing in.

'She couldn't have seen it coming'.
'She wouldn't have felt a thing'.
'Could you please I.D. the body'.
What the hell was happening?

So I arranged a baby-sitter
And I went down to that place
Where they had stored her body,
Pulled a sheet over her face.

'That's her'. I numbly muttered
And signed on dotted lines.
Made arrangements for a funeral,
And cried alone sometimes.

Perhaps I'll see you later.
Perhaps I'll be OK.
Perhaps I'll open up the door
And join you there one day.

Tears stain my pillow

Tears stain my pillow, though no one else shall see.
The one who shared my pillow, no longer lives with me.

Such simple words, 'no longer lives' but why must they be true?
I whisper to my pillow 'You know I still love you'.

An empty bed, an empty life, an emptiness untold.
A life that's without meaning, without you to hold.

Forgive me. Love me. Hold me. Your soul enwrap me please.
Free me from my torment, my heart I beg appease.

I loved you then. I love you now. My love will ever be.
Tears stain my pillow, though no one else shall see.

Always

I watched you sitting quietly,
framed in sunlight.
I wondered what large thoughts
had carved a frown on so small a face.
Were you mulling deep philosophies?
Or counting dust motes in the air?
Or lost in a reverie that an adult
can only recall through gauze-wrapped memories?

I watched and took a snapshot with my mind,
telling myself to remember you that way - always.
And I do.
And I shall.
Always.

A Life

musty room
grimy walls
papers scattered

unpaid bills
stamped
with coffee cup rings

none of these things
tell your story

only the ripped
photograph jigsaw puzzle
holds a clue
as to what ailed you

the rusty razor blade
that traced your wrists
show that which killed you

as you sprawl
in pallid repose
framed in crimson
you remain
an enigma

Echoes

The restless night cries out amid whimpers from my slumber
And all I wake to hear are the echoes of your words.
Dawn is breaking lightly, casting light onto my darkness
As the morning chorus chatters with the gossip of the birds.

Each time your name I whisper, to hear your sweet 'Good Morning'
But as always only silence echoes empty from the walls.
And the waking desolation of my life grows ever stronger
There's no answer from my lover to my heart-felt, plaintive calls.

You are no more. Extant in me. No more gracing others' worlds.
Just echoes of a life well-loved, and the pain in which I'm wreathed.
I said our love would burn forever. Did you doubt me then?
I told the truth (though I knew it not) with every word I breathed.

Rest in peace my darling, you live on inside my dreams
And all I wait to hear are the echoes of your words.
Dawn is breaking lightly, casting light onto my darkness
As the morning chorus chatters with the gossip of the birds.

Tell me, please

Does he caress your skin?
And smell your hair?
Don't tell me, please
I don't want to know.

Does he whisper soft words?
And make you laugh?
Don't tell me, please
I don't want to know.

Does he hold your hand?
And kiss your eyes?
Don't tell me, please
I don't want to know.

Does he sing you songs?
And spend the night?
Don't tell me, please
I don't want to know.

Does he love you?
As I loved you?

No tincture for a broken heart

I sit a-bed with sheets disgruntled
Head in hands and briny-browed
Rewind-replay the tragic mindscapes
Of a love now disavowed

Days and weeks and months keep passing
Still no torments' ending near
And the clock of time keeps ticking
Counting off each empty year

So each night I wake rememb'ring
The day that you were laid to rest
As the demons prowl the darkness
Clawing at my mind-undressed

One day I'll sleep until the morning
Without recalling we're apart
But now the wound is raw and aching
No tincture for a broken heart

Backward Glance

Time will tell the time to tell the time.
Time is to be spent not to be read.
Time will tell the time to tell the time.
Time will tell the dead man he is dead.

When autumn welcomes winter's frosty brow
And lusty youth's been doused by passing years.
When life long lived is viewed from 'here and now'
What time is left to dry your salty tears?

What use is knowing at the very end
That all you've said and done amounts to naught?
Except the love of those that you call friend;
How bittersweet the love that is not bought.

For once surveyed so much is left undone.
So much that's done that cannot be put right.
So carry your regrets, but do not run.
Just walk headlong toward the last 'Goodnight'.

I sit these nights

I sit these nights
Embroidering thoughts on the velveteen darkness of my room;
Weaving tapestries of days gone by;
Picking out the melancholy memories of my life;
Gazing at the soft under-belly of the soul.

I sit these nights
Alone.
So alone.
So terribly
alone.

She Glanced At Me

She glanced at me
and did not see
the lovelight burn inside of me.

She glanced at me
and did not know
how I longed to love her so.

She glanced at me
and did not care
how much I dreamed of kissing her.

She glanced at me
and walked away
I love her still unto this day.

She glanced at me
and did not see
and did not know
and did not care
and walked away.

Valarie Vandegriff (moonflower)

Beckville, Texas USA

I am a married stay-at-home mom with 3 teenagers still 'in the nest'. I currently live in east Texas, but I was born in California and grew up in Oklahoma, Kansas, Missouri, and Arkansas. I've been writing poetry for approximately 5 years. Family, Nature, and life in general, are constant sources of inspiration to me...a fact for which I am eternally grateful.

Stardancing

i wanna go where the night goes
stardancing across the endless sky
i wanna know what the night knows
and be enlightened with moondust in my eyes

i wanna feel the gentle nightwinds song
caressing my skin soft and slow
i wanna peer into nights misty dawn
and be enchanted by her magic show

i wanna hear the music of the night
as it sings the earth to sleep
i wanna dream along in nights moonlight
and know the dreams are mine to keep

untethered

the leaves go floating
past my window
fluttering, swirling,
wending their way
through this crispy day..
now captured by a
bold puff of wind
that wants to play,
they go skipping and
dancing..whirling away
playing hide and seek
with the sassy breeze..
they look like
they're having fun..
untethered
from their trees

beside the sea

walking beside the sea alone
walking slowly through the sand
i see a shell and pick it up
i love the feel
of it in my hands
i marvel at the beauty of
this treasure from the sea
so smooth and cool and
beautiful...i have to
take it home with me!

playing the game

everywhere on the wide world's web
faceless identities travel on-line
nameless and voiceless they click and connect
while searching for something they hope they'll find

naive' souls are captured by the web
becoming addicted to its magic
they surf the pages and play online
letting others become what they imagine

chat rooms with user-friendly tools
can produce perfection in a flash
typed words create the perfect face
imagination supplies bodies to match

innocent young ones chat in these rooms
where players and cyber-games abound
then with a click they return to reality
dreaming about what they think they've found..

..a storm..

the night was humid, with sweltering heat
the air was heavy, stagnate
the very atmosphere felt charged..
as if it were waiting..expectant..

as storm clouds brew in the smouldering sky
a hushed eerie stillness settles over the town..
it creates a mood;..strange, surreal,
a night suspended...spellbound..

through the steamy haze a stranger walks
rugged, tall, strong..he warily watches
the churning sky..it reflects how he feels on this
stormy night...restless, tense...dissatisfied..

mopping sweat from his neck, once again he
pushes on..empty inside and alone, going
nowhere, but moving on...like the gathering
momentum of the distant storm..

she sits unseen beneath the trees
moody, sticky from the heat
she sighs, longing for a
whiff of air...a breeze..

feeling the tremors of the rumbling sky
she watches in awe as it transforms..
its turbulence is reflected in her eyes as
she watches and awaits the approaching storm..

on this sizzling night they were both alone
two hungry souls with needy hearts
hearts alive, but beating in frozen
shells, hard...like stone..

caught in the aura of the pulsating sky
their souls connect as eyes meet eyes
both pairs instantly attracted..
captured..magnetized..

kindled by the heat of the evolving storm
two hearts are softened and a bond is
formed..the icy shells slowly melt..
the thaw silent, unseen...but felt..

underneath the ominous squall, he slowly
walks to where she stands, and as the rain
begins to fall he smiles at her..
then he holds out his hand..

as the storm explodes in the ignited sky, she
smiles back..hesitant, shy.. but, she takes his
hand..tonight she's just a woman, he's just a man
she doesnt care if its wrong..tomorrow she'll care..
yes tomorrow..after the storm has gone..

dancing in the sunlight

sky so clear and blue
clouds marshmallow white
birds singing their songs
breezes blowing exactly right
butterflies and dragonflies
flitting round about
you and me smiling
dancing in the sunlight..

thunderstorm

sticky humid air
stifling unmoving
distant rumblings
gather momentum
as squall-line moves
ever nearer

disturbance brewing
with wind gusts
and lightening flashes
churning masses collide
producing noisy
thunderclashes

storm-darkened sky
crackling, vibrating
blows the fronts
both cold and warm
to their final
destination..
thunderstorm is born!

Autumn sings..

Autumn, in all her glory,
sings to me the secret
she's known all along:
that the circle of life is
turning, moving,
changing the singers..
but not the song

once again

rain falls
cold gray
night comes
ending day
all alone
yet again
loves gone
life ends
sun rises
day begins
hope returns
earth spins
love lives..
once again

money

greenbacked wishes
talking floating bouncing
always burning holes in pockets
paper

overload

muscles: aching, strained
illusion: no pain, no gain
fact: more pain than gain!

close enough..

she picks up her guitar
and twangs out some chords..
to her its anger-management,
a way to cope..and she says
it keeps her sane
when she's bored..

she's young and strong but
she thinks her life is going
nowhere, so she plays her pain
with a pick and some strings..
plunking out heart wrenching
notes and tunes of despair..

i wish i could ease her pain
while she lives her 'growing pains'
i wish i could make her see
that her dreams are not
just 'pie in the sky'
i wish she could see herself
through my eyes..

she has what it takes to live
her dreams..inborn determination
to be the best, combined with
learning skills razor-sharp..
but we only see what she
chooses to express..

she hides herself behind
her eyes..what is she afraid of?
why doesn't she want the world
to see and know her beautiful
but undiscovered soul?

music is her favorite world,
it's a way of escaping..it's her
place to go when things get tough..
she tunes life out, then strums
her feelings with her fingers..
it's not perfect..but for her
it's close enough..

a simple smile

the music is playing
they look at each other
from across the room
they smile their special smile
their eyes are wordlessly
saying it all..that yes
the dance has been worthwhile

she wonders as she smiles at him
if he already knows, that
even now after all these years
he's still her true real-life hero
as he gazes back and winks at her,
another one of their special signs,
he wishes they could be alone and
he plays the scene in his mind

they've faced the music together
in life's eternal dance, bending
its notes into harmonious sounds
sometimes gliding, sometimes falling,
sometimes just dancing round and round
their eyes now meeting..saying again
that yes it has been worthwhile
all mutually conveyed to each other
in a single simple smile

we danced

twilight advances softly
across the vacant beach
i follow her dancing shadows
to the edge of the playful sea

deepening blue horizens
far as my eyes can see
dark sea and dark sky melding
blending in perfect harmony

quiet thoughts meander
drifting in and out like the waves
sea's rhythm dancing softly
to the tune Mother Nature plays

soothing aura surrounds us all
the sky the sea and me
it beckons me to dance along
inviting me to take the lead

so i skip across the crystal sand
waltzing with the teasing waves
i touch the sky with outstretched arms
welcoming her soft embrace

the mighty sea and the majestic sky
created their magic stage for me
and on this night we danced as one
the sky the sea and me

chat that!

with tears in her eyes
she asks me(her mother)to listen
while she explains the
latest chatworld transmissions, so
i hold her close, feeling her pain
while her tears fall down...
(like slow steady rain!)
she talks about how you so
cleverly disguised
those unspoken truths...
(otherwise known as lies!)
with practiced maneuvers
designed to deceive her...
(and oh man..was she a believer!)
she said your words were so smooth
and your promises were golden...
(yep..before she knew it her heart was stolen!)
she loved you online
enlisting her keypad, and
to her it was real, so
she virtually gave you everything
that she had...
(never dreaming it would turn out bad!)
but now the truth is finally out
her make believe days are through
she knows now it was just a game...
(and she KNOWS that she WILL get over you!)
and guess what!..here in the 'real' world
she's still exactly who she was
before she knew you!
yes she's still exactly the same
as she was before CHAT...
(but she IS a little wiser..
so she thanks you for that!)

words.. unforgotten

the words were like arrows
pointed and sharp
they pierced deep and
became forever embedded
in my heart
never to be forgotten
or removed
but just living there
as if they somehow knew
that time
was on their side..

Winter's gift

Winter arrives softly
with gentle flakes of falling snow
she's beautifying Mother Nature's face
in the only way that she knows..

silently she works her magic
painting the land in purest white
giving it as a gift from her heart
sending it down throughout the night

then, gift-wrapped in dawns box of bluest sky
and tied with gold ribbons from the sun,
Winter offers her tribute..and she smiles
as Mother Nature softly whispers..'well done!'

standing here

i stand alone
erect and tall
unable to move
i cant walk,
cant even crawl..
i surround you
in silence
week after week
for i cannot even speak
i listen in secret
to your sobs..
its a secret i keep
like a haunting
sad song
my eyes see everything
and these ears..yes
they hear it all
but i can do nothing..
nothing but stand
here, frozen, through
it all..i have no voice
im only the walls..

..my garden grows..

ripe sun-scorched melons
fruit fermenting on the vine
watermelon wine

has anybody got a pencil?

in my lifetime
i bet i've spent
hundreds of dollars
on pencils and pens
cuz i write ALL the time
(from the a.m. to the p.m.)..
and in our house where
there's three school-age kids
(who i'm always and always buying
pencils for-over and over again!)...
wouldn't you kinda think that a pencil could
be found..at least.. just.. every now and then?..

cyber reality

on-line you can
shout out loud
without making
a sound,
you can fall
in love without
sharing a kiss,
you can travel
anywhere without
leaving your chair,
you can be a hero
(even if your a zero!)
you can build
castles in the sky
....but....
you cant see
if the truth
is in someone's eyes..

side by side

i love being
beside the sea,
heeding the oceans voice,
as it rushes ashore
with secrets for me..
secrets that waft
into my ears,
secrets that only i
am able to hear..
with every caress
of the constant tide,
the mighty sea and i
become intertwined,
bonded by time
forever linked
hand-to-hand,
the sea is water...
i am the sand

stargazing

hushed dark starry night
velvety canvas with lights
i gaze..mesmerized

liquid gold

flowers
bees
honey

midnight waltz

the Night approaches softly
falling gently on the land
caressing Earth's blooming fields
and flowered lawns as it
gathers them up in its arms

Earth's face is slowly changed
by the fragile touch of Night's
magic wand as expanding
shadows embrace the terrain
in this nightly liaison

Earth graces the air with fragrant
perfume and patiently watches
as Night hangs up the moon then
sprinkles an endless supply of
twinkling stars across the sky

dressed in her best evening costume
Earth now composes sweet music
for this recurring nocturnal rendezvous
it hums and buzzes in the background
singing to Night in live surround-sound

hidden eyes and ears observe
the presentation that occurs..
installed at the very beginning of time
it plays out night after night
as Night and Earth intertwine

at last all is ready
the midnight stage is set
and it waits for romance..
Night tenderly looks at Earth
then softly chants..lets dance..lets dance..

clicking start

two people living in separate places
scrolling through sites on the worlds wide web
browsing in rooms where names have no faces
searching for someone with whom to connect

then with a 'click' they both are logged in
instantly linked for the very first time
chatting and bridging the distance within
kindred souls touching..becoming entwined

connected invisibly, they tread space and time
each touched by words from silent lips
words transported to each other on-line..
transported by flying fingertips

now they are united within the webs maze
bound to each other heart-to-heart
two people together on the 'nets highways'
two souls who touched..just by clicking start..

snowfall

white work of art
sifting wafting drifting
a winter wonderland ballet
peaceful

transformation

springtime breezes
gentle, soft
kissing the earths
changing face,
touching the land
and the rocks,
as winter's grip
evaporates..

sunwarmed landscapes
profuse, green
evolving into spring
they're letting go
of winters hold
..transforming..
allowing the sun
to steal the show

newborn flowers
untouched, fresh
gracing the earth's
valleys and hills
spreading their colors
with finesse'
as mother earth
changes her dress..

the hunted

shadowed pond ripples,
hunted ones become hunters
fishing for supper

..its Friday!..

16 year-old daughter, getting ready to meet her 'steady'
calls to me from her side of the bathroom door:
"Mom can you find me my pink sweater?..i think its in the dryer!"
my other 16 year-old daughter, with plans of her own
is calling me from school on her cell phone:
"Mom basketball practice was cancelled, i need a ride home!"
14 year-old son comes breezin in, all excited:
"Mom! Mom i need money!..Ron wants me to go to the
movies with him!"
ahhh ...the week-end begins...

dancing the dream

the stage is lit
the dancers are ready
the moment is here
they enter..slow but steady

the music plays
they begin thier routine
spinning twirling..dancers
living their dreams

they gracefully bow
then leave the stage
the lights are dimmed
and the music fades

now they cry..tears of
joy on each face
the votes are in..
they won 1st place!

..words..

powerful, strong
changing minds
righting wrongs
moving hearts
causing smiles
removing doubts
making peace
bridging miles
bittersweet
everlasting
producing prose
making rhyme
imparting hope
spanning time
composing song
soothing balm
...words...

Naushin Walji (friend_forever)

Dar es Salaam, Tanzania

My name is Naushin, call me Nosh or friend or Naush... currently 21 years old and living in Dar es Salaam Tanzania, East Africa. Writing just happened by luck at high school, and I have been writing since.

Mom

Dearest mom...
I thank you from the bottom of my heart...
Without you, I would not have been here, on this earth...
I am sorry for the pain I caused you
...During my birth, a lot you went through...
The nine months you kept me in your womb,
Keeping me safe and secured...
Away from all harm...
Thank you for giving me your blood,
Your energy and your food,
You are the reason I am grown up today,
For without you, I would have been an unborn baby...
Thank you for the pains you took,
Ensuring that I was educated to the best of your ability...
Thank you for the enormous support you gave...
Let me assure you, your hugs went a long way...
Thank you for understanding
...When I had no time for you...
Thank you for sharing and caring,
When I couldn't take care of myself
Thanks for your shoulder...
The one I cried on,
When I was overcome with grief...
Thank you for making things right,
For making me believe...
Thank you for all your efforts
In making me what I am today,
I really love you, Mom...
Cause, Like wine...
You get better with age everyday!!
Love you, Mom

Give Me Your Today

A shiver rushes through my spine
As tenderly your lips circle mine
Tongues play an erotic dance of their own
As both minds are lost in elation.

Fingers crossing, holding hands forever
Lost in the moment of the ecstatic tremor.

Lost dreamily into each other's eyes
... How can I control what my body desires?
See how perfectly we fit together
As if our bodies were meant for each other.

Caress my features, set your desires free
Let your fingers roam unreservedly across what belongs to thee

Oh! If this be sin
Let me be a sinner
Oh! If this be an offence
Let me be an offender.

Let them talk, those who may
Just spend time with me, give me your today

Hold me against your beating heart
Show me the rhythm of your heartbeat
I want to listen to it beating my name
To hear that you love me the same.

Lick my dry lips moist...
Cover my mouth with yours when I scream in pleasure.

Bring happy tears to my eye
Then gently wipe them away
Tell me you love me
Do this gently and kiss me...

Poisonous Memories Call Me

Just one small sms* "call me"
Opened a floodgate of emotions
The reminiscences that I never wished to remember
Forgotten tears,
Which I hoped would never shine through again
Just a small call me
Changed the weather to stormy.

The times best left in the past
Flooded back to haunt my today
The memories covered with cobwebs
Rushed right back
When I had almost succeeded in locking them away
Why... Why did you have to sms me?
I was happy in my own darkened slumber of dreams.

Just one phone call
And I was a broken hearted girl again
Thinking about how deceived I had felt
How much I always loved you
And how you left me...

Broken pieces of my heart lay scattered on the floor
As I was pleading for you to stay...
To not leave me empty...
You left me crying on the same bed we had made love
You left with my heart torn...
Void of any emotion
Yet I couldn't help but think of you every day
Mumbled your name before I would go to bed
Think about you every morning when I wake up...

You promised, didn't you?
That we would be together forever?
That was 6 years ago
When our relationship had just begun...

You murdered my spirit slowly
Like a lingering poison killing one softly
Thoughts about you destroyed me a little daily
Why? Why did you have to call?
Why did you have to go away?
Why couldn't you just stay?
I missed you so much every day.

Just one sms this morning
Threw me back in time to the beginning
6 years of self-therapy
Useless books on psychology
I am back in a place I first started off with
Back in that darkened hole I had finally come out of
With a terribly suicidal state of mind I had left behind.

Self-loathe and hatred rush through my veins again
Revolted at myself for still longing for your arms
Disgusted that I will still take you back
After all you've done...

SMS - Short Messaging Service - Cellular Text messages

I'll Be There

Whenever you are down
I will help you put away your frown...
When I cannot...I will lay down beside you
And just listen...I'll be there...

I will be the one person you can count on
I will hold your hand through times of trial
I will rekindle your love through my hug and smile

If it hurts to look back
And you are too scared to look ahead
Look beside you, I'll be there...

And I will always be here
Waiting right here
To catch you if you fall
I can't tell you why I care this much
I will be there, is all I can swear...

When you need support to rise
Look out... My hand will always be outstretched
I will walk with you through every step of your life
I will support you, when your feet fail to carry your burden...
I will be there... forever...

When you need to stay in darkness and think
I will be there, with my candle and matches
I will sit with you in the dark,
I will think with you in the night
And when you are ready to see the light
My candle I will light
...I will be there...

I will give you my strength... I will make you strong
I will shield you from the world's biggest storm
I will love you... I will keep you safe and warm...
You don't even need to ask... I will be there.

When you are scared, lost and losing ground
I will always be around...
I will push you to the top...
I will give you the will to carry on,
I'll be there, with all I've got...

Whenever you are overcome with grief
When your eyes cry with strife
I'll be there... crying with you... in your grief

When you need to talk
Or just take an early morning walk
I will be there... Listening to what you've got to say
I will be there... All the time... All the way...

"To the world you may be one person
But, to one person you may be the world..."
So next time you say nobody cares
Remember... I'll always be there...

When the Grass Was Green

Remembering the day we first bumped into each other
When the grass was green on the hills yonder...
While the thunder rumbled across a distance
And somewhere over the rainbow
An angel played with her halo
I slipped and fell...
Wishing for the luck of a leprechaun
I fell into your arms... the love story had begun

Looking into each others' eyes
Colored lips... red like a blush on a rose
As the sun awakes, yawns and rubs its eyes
Rays of love shine through, as the sun gives us his daily dose

After seventeen years of being together
After being with you almost forever
Wordless, and faceless
You desert me, left me feeling shapeless and soulless

Just like the rusty hinges swing the slowest
The memories stay on in our hearts the longest
As our loved ones slowly leave the world
We live on, cursing our very existence into the earth.
Leaving with them, If we ever could.

Pearls of Memories

Pearls of memories
One by one fall from my eye
Recalling the bygone stories
Remembering you and I

Hallucinations trouble my vision
These images displayed at the back of my mind
Holding your hand, seeing your hand in mine
Lips meeting lips, stealing those moments from time
Those imaginaries that lie in my imagination...

These torments ache in my very soul...
Those times spent with you leave me with a deep hole
Burning fires within my heart
Where is he, who has left his name in my very breath?

Alas! These painful pearls of memories...
Forever left etched in my soul
Never again, will I ever be whole
Leaving watery marks on these ageing pages...

For my friends...

As I walk down the halls
Looking at the graffiti on the walls
As I approach various rooms
I watch the flowers bloom
I see a variety of people
All very, very special

Berlie, Heinzs, Ven and Tom Watson
All have suites in the top floor
The conference room reserved for elders
That's where they mostly are...

Important discussions, family squabbles and general enemy attacks
They sort out all the serious issues

Tom's suite is done in whites
And he has a special place in our hearts
He advises us when we are wrong
And boosts us up in spirits when we loose faith in ourselves.

Heinzs turned half his set of rooms into his lab
He is the one you go to when you loose your key to the house
He is the one who has extra sets of keys to all the rooms
A very busy man, but always around when you need anything done
He is our pops, loving, strict, friendly and wise.

Mama Berlie is the head of the house
She is always around,
Has own set of rooms, that's always unlocked
Knock before you enter though,
She is mostly on her computer,
Earning bread to keep up the home

Ven is the chief of all those police people around
She monitors the people who monitor the home
Make sure nobody is up to any kind of mischief
She makes sure that there is no kind of unfair play
And sometimes gets into mischief of her own.

Darkness approaches the dimly lit halls
I catch a glimpse of thief of dreams
Walking in and out of rooms
Taking away the nightmares,
Replacing them with pleasant, sweet dreams

Butterflies's room is close by...
As I peek in, I see a rainbow of colors
All different colored wings
Yellow walls, Blue ceiling
With her baby alligators... And her weird reptiles
She is happy in her own sweet world...

Oh, I glimpse Preston disappearing into the Lady's room
Wonder what he wants from that pretty one's home
Oh, I get it now, her secret stash of beer hidden under her bed?
Or does he want to steal her stick again?

VivaldiFall's room is almost always empty
He is in the army, you see...
A man in uniform
With a good heart and soul
He is around sometimes
To check up on how well behaved we all are

Blaze's door is colored blue, with silver stars stuck on them
Her room is full of faerie dust *cough*
Seems like she is cleaning the stars again in her room
Silently waving a goodbye, I close the doors and walk by

Debbie, She's just joined the home
She's all the way from Canada
She has a great style of words
And her head is always bowed in prayer
She prays for all of us, and is closer to God.

Haroo is another lost, wandering soul
He is around, never leaving his room
His heart aches, His soul pains
Yet, he is a great friend, and one you would wish you had.

Moonflower, what would I do without you
You love reading a lot, and writing Haiku
She lives near the end of the hallway
Her room has paintings of beautiful flowers
Orchids, roses and moonflowers

And the list would be incomplete
If I fail to mention Gillian
She shapes up poetry, keeps it really sexy
She is the chancellor of the pages
Gives the Great LadyS a run for her money.

People come, people go
But friends come, take your heart
And leave footsteps in your life forever

Great huge hugs to each and every one of you...
Nine hundred members, all so special
All so precious...
Its true, what would I have done without you
What would I have been, had I not met you all...
A mad human, living in a cell with padded walls
Love you all.

Two Lost Souls

Two souls
Lost,
Wandering in the night.

Two souls...
Whom should they tell their plight?

Two souls,
Lonely...
Tired...
Confused
Looking for company.

Two lost ones
Looking for loved ones...

Two souls,
Brought together by similar circumstances...
Two souls,
Torn between the two worlds.

Two tired, helpless young ones
... Suffering from emotional disorders...
The domestic lives in chaotic disarrays...

Two saddened persons...
Living with terrible fathers
Tortures follow them throughout...

Two lost souls
... Wandering in the worlds...
Lost, tired and burnt out
With nobody to hear them out
Nobody to love them
To care for them
Or to cherish them.

Two souls,
Lost
... Wandering in the night...

Another Weepy Old Missing You Poem

Whenever I close my eyes...
I can always see your face

My hand reaches out to you
... But always you disappear without a clue

I search for your hand
... But even a glimpse I can not find

I yearn to touch you again
But your face is always washed away by the rain...
Why else do you think I feel so much pain?

Misty waters cloud my visions
... As I begin regretting my decisions...

Today my side is empty...
Because I just wont let you be...

Yesterday...
You wanted to be with me...
I turned you away from me

When you asked for my love...
All I gave was a laugh...

Oh Lord... I misunderstood him...
All I knew was just a bad dream

Because of that... I kept you away...
Why did I not listen to you that day?

Today realized you were right
The things were said out of spite...

I let you go...
Why... I don't know...

You were just sharing your fears...
But I misunderstood your tears...

You were helpless with your pain...
I thought you were doing it for personal gain

You are now gone...
Boy... am I so alone...

Across the seven seas...
I search for your trace...

You are nowhere to be found...
And I am tired of looking around

Where are you...
So lonely here... What shall I do?

As if in a trance...
I beg for a second chance...

A Friend

A friend is someone, whom you can trust,
depend on,
and can count on in difficult times.

A friend is someone who shares your laughter, sadness, sorrows,
dreams and your nightmares.

A friend is someone,
who can bring a smile to your face, when you are sad,
who could give you a hug when things look bad,
who is there for you,
when everybody else is not!

A friend is someone who is gentle, kind and loving...
to help you through your worst times.

A friend is someone who offers you a hand,
when others show you their backs...

A friend is someone,
who wipes tears off your eyes,
but doesn't shade them.

A friend is all that
...and a lot more

For My Guardian Angel

Every time I try,
Thinking surely I deserve a second shot
I fail...on the spot
I don't really know why.

I don't really care now anymore
I will probably just stay here and grieve over
From deep underneath, from the core of my being...
No more chances... I swear, no more.

Every smile that I give
Bring more and more angst
Every relationship I make
Turns sour, and many hearts break.

Any word spoken by my cursed lips
Tears you apart...
My guardian angel it kills...

Oh why... why do I say stuff
Why cant I just f***kin be silent?
As tears cloud my sight
And I finally begin seeing clearly...
It's not their fault... it is more than likely me.

Frustrated, tired and beaten...
With my head down...
With my teary eyes and saddened soul
I move away, silently into my shell.

Disheartened and desolate...
I wait for my guardian angel
To make it all right...
To bring me back to life...

An Era... No More...

To have loved and gone astray
Hearts broken and left for display
Staring at the photographs by my bedside
Remembering why you aren't by my side
Noticing a sudden wetness on my pale cheeks
Bottled up feelings, reminiscing those last few weeks...

Flashback
Into another time...
A world happy and sublime
That has now become lonesome and pitch-black

Loosing myself
Falling badly
...The devil himself
Torturing me relentlessly
Smiling through the ache
I feel the heartbreak

Sleep eluded me that night
Restlessly wishing for my knight
Your face surrounded by the dark
You step forth into the light
Handing me a greeting card from Hallmark
You say, "Spend hours with me tonight..."

Nodding in accent
Ending my torment
Your lips encircle mine
As our bodies intertwine
Hands freely roaming my curves
Completely unsettling my shrill nerves

Arousing emotions no one has done before
Needing your caresses and touch

Wanting you more
Yet...
Unsure.

You left me stranded ashore
Left like you don't care anymore
I cried until I could cry no more
Feeling abused; confused; depressed and like a whore

Cut my wrists out of desperation
The need to end it all

Bleeding on the floor
Last moments before I close the door
Wondering why I loved... where I lost it all
Fighting the urge to let go... staring at your picture on my bedside

Taking my last breath, I whisper your name
As mister death takes my soul
My lifeless body aflame
An era
In time
No more.

Together Asunder

Listen to what the heart wants to say
You love him... the memories have not gone astray
Whenever the mind plays
...Those games always

Oh stop being Naïve child...
Stop with the Denials
Your heart fluttered the moment he smiled
Your heartbeats stop at the sound of his chuckles

A frown wrinkles my brow
Why I love you, I honestly do not know
My mind trying to bring up those images
The gates with the rusty hinges
The house, colored the very lightest blue
The steps leading to the mahogany door
The feeling when all that was still new...

Trying to run past the good times
...So that I can come to the bad ones
Trying to run away from memories of the lifetimes
... I so desperately want to blame...
I start again, those blaming games...

It wasn't me... It wasn't you
What was it then?
That sliced our relationship into two...

Still have that poster...
When we both posed for that picture
Photographs forever capturing the smiling us
Why is there then no more us...

You are now you,
I am now me...
We seem to have lost our "we"

Was this even meant to be?
What's going on?
Where have we reached in place and time...
Can we not go back to the world we left behind?

For A Brother So Sweet

Faheem... My dearest brother
...For like you, there's none other

I love you from deep down
And I feel Sad... Whenever you frown

Your smile drives my monsters away
... About your unending reassurance... What can I say?

Your laughter is pure music to my ears
And I am thankful for all the 20 years...

You keep me happy daily
With your loving banter and frolic

You bring me chocolates when I am down
And cheer me up, whenever I frown

You keep away my foes
... And keep away my tears

You are a brother so sweet
You... are my gift from god...
My little treat...
He promised me in his abode...

You make life fun for me...
And Am I glad... Your are always here for me!

Every time I think about the love we share
And always... the way you care...

You are the most handsome young man in Tanzania
And I know... that you know you are...

I pray to god that you are happy always
And that you are successful in all your endeavours...

Thomas Watson (Tom Watson)

Novato, California USA

One of the more senior members of the Poetry Pages, Tom Watson has been writing off and on for over fifty years. During that time he has served in and retired from the U.S. Air Force, been married and widowed, been sober for over 30 years and saved by our Lord and Savior, Jesus Christ, for over 2 years. He has authored his own book of poetry and prose, titled *Between Shadows and the Light*, available at amazon.com and barnesandnoble.com. He has also contributed to the following publications from Poetrypages.com: *Poetry Pages Vol II*; *Poetry from the Dark Side*; *Within Three Lines*, and *Lost and Found*.

Shhhh... Listen

Shhh...Listen... can you hear?
That sound, as the blade opened a new window...
Was that a moan from your
Lips, or the winds of the future
Closing tomorrow's door?
Wait, I think that sound
Isn't only the splash of blood
Falling on the floor or ground,
But the tears of your future;
Of chances and friends you're
Missing with each crimson drop,
Each second you fail to stop...
This symphony of life running
Away from future sunnings;
And possible change and laughter;
Away from other loves, and, after
Time, maybe a family of sons and daughters,
And the possibility to bring home a friend,
Who, like you, couldn't hear
The sound of possibilities, drip, drip, dripping
To the drain of life's end.

Let Go

Your fingers are closed
In a grip so tight!
Why?!

Inside your soul
You hold your pain with all your might...
Why?!

Your heart constricts;
Your life is restricted,
All joy is disconnected...
Why?

Does it give you pleasure
To bleed from your soul?
Is it satisfying to measure
Your life in messed up goals?

Open those fingers
In which your heart is sealed...
Let Go!

Remove those nails
Let yourself heal...
Let Go!

Grab His hand instead..
Seal the gashes where your soul bleeds,
Feel the quiet in your head,
Know the joy of a life freed...

Listen to the anguish of His voice,
Of a pain much harsher than yours.
Borne to His death, in loving choice,
That you, we, need not die with ours.

Now look at your life
No longer living on the edge of a knife...
Let Go!

Open your heart in peace
Raise your eyes from your pain...
Let go!

How sad, time spent lost in tears
Lost in a tightness bound
By a past of long suffered fears
So easily forgotten in the Love just found.

Let go...there is nothing of yours to hold
Of sorrow, loneliness, or pain.
Let go...release it to the one God, so bold,
To come, as a man, to save you from suffering again.

Unfinished

You whispered into the darkness;
And the breeze shifted the mist;
You threw into the limpid water a kiss;
And the ripples returned what was missed...

Smiles, when nothing was said;
Peace, in an empty bed;
Purpose to a life once thought dead;
Hope for a new sunrise ahead.

You laughed at my silliness;
You held my hand through my pain;
You calmed my angriness
You sheltered me from life's rains...

But-
Then
I awakened

.

.

To a silence still spoken;
And I knew, again, what you took,
When you went away with our unfinished book.

Whisper to Me

Whisper to me
Call me to your distant shore;
Speak softly of where I need to be
Pull my soul to where it was once before......

On the side of the road I watch
Your messenger slowly retreat
From its nightly incursion to this spot
Where your power stretches to reach.
I hear your call and drive away to follow
Out of town, passing mist covered lake;
Where morning mist hovers in the valley hollow,
And peace is given for mated swans to partake

Whisper to me
With your salted scent
Invade my mind, gently
Wrap me with your beauty's hint......

Passing more picnic grounds where
Only a deer and fawn graze peacefully
Their own picnic on dewy grass, unaware
Of the power and beauty that awaits me.
While the messenger fog backs away still
I wind around hills and valleys, velvet brown
Tendrils of grey beckoning with secrets to tell
Till on my final climb I view the surrendered ground...

Whisper to me now
In your softly muted roar
Of power and beauty endowed
And crashing crescendo of your shore....

Majestic blue and green, white foam flecks;
Stretch mightily to the fading grey sky
Then fall forward upon the long sandy neck,

Caressing it gently, molding it as time goes by.
To see such power and gentleness, in turn,
I marvel as the whispering surrounds my soul,
Entwining me in magic, making my heart forever to yearn
For sights, sounds and wind blown spray, seen from this sandy
knoll...

Whisper to me..
Call me to your distant shore;
Speak softly of where I need to be
Pull my soul to where it was once before......

Walking The Dog

While out today, walking the dog,
Watching her sniffing a post,
A patch of grass, pieces of rotten log,
I saw myself through the Holy Ghost.

I realized the love held by the leash's tug;
The concern for her not to be left to roam;
I knew how the Word guides me with gentle hugs,
Through encouraging wisdom, leading me home.

At the side of the path we took
Was a swath of brown grass, trees and brush
A fence near there close to a little brook,
Where her approach caused disturbance of the moment's hush.

I saw these distractions as things in my world,
That drew me from the intended path's direction
Where, in my exploring, were brought new chances to unfurl;
While His love maintained my course, without my perception.

We continued on, her wandering wanting to stray,
And, without that leash, I know she would run,
Leaving me to watch nervously and pray
No car or truck would find her and ruin her fun.

Isn't life such as this? All along
Pulling us to run free of restraints;
Drawing us to things that are dark and generally wrong,
To live and be dead away from His word's constraints?

The leash pulled tight, bringing me from my thoughts;
She had decided to wander toward the street.
A gentle tug to remind her she should not,
And she happily returned to keep pace at my feet...

Temptation, in the same way as new adventures
Tries to draw me from Him and away from His goal for me
Then I am reminded, by the tug of His Words
Of His love that leads where the path moves peacefully.

Each day, as best I can, I grab the leash in hand
And together we wander, over grass, over rock
Sometimes we may take a trek on the sea's sand,
Keeping the lead loose, keeping her close, to encourage with my
talk.

In my prayers, I ask Him to guide me each day,
To take me on the path or road He has set for me;
Knowing He will guide my steps regardless of what lay in my way,
Held by His loving word, I am restrained and I am free.

Splinter

I have this splinter
Of ancient wood
Burrowing within
And it feels so good!

It is just a sliver,
Sliding into my heart;
A life saver...
Giving me a whole new start...

Wood so old;
Of a love so bold;
From Calvary's cross
Embedded, at such a cost...

Once near a nail
Once near a tear...
Once near a nail
Once near a tear...

I have this sliver,
This piece of eternal grace,
This peace of forever,
And I am humbled by its starting place;

Washed, from a cross of pain,
By our Lord's tears and rain,
It slid into my soul, in the flood
Of His sacrificial blood.

Wood so old
Of a love so bold
From Calvary's cross
Embedded at such a cost

Once near a nail
Once near a tear...

Once near a nail...
Once near a tear

I have this splinter
Of Ancient wood
Burrowed within,
And it feels so good.

It is just a sliver,
That slid into my heart
A life saver
Gave me a whole new start...

Wood so old;
Of a love so bold;
From Calvary's cross
Embedded, at such a cost...

Once near a nail
Once near a tear...

Once near a nail...
Once near a tear

A Short Walk

I took a short walk
Away from the memories and pain
To a place where I could talk.

The sky was blue, the sea like a gem
As slow moving clouds, grey bordered puffs of white,
Shadowed me while thinking of what to ask Him.

The path I was walking upon
Was edged by weeds and golden flowers,
Leaving me more needful to walk on.

Suddenly the trail narrowed on a slopping grade;
I held near-by branches of strong oak trees,
Knowing, with each slide, my purpose could not fade.

At the bottom of the hill,
I saw a blue-jay, lying on a mound of grass;
And through my tears, my purpose grew still.

On I walked, passing a small pond,
With its songs of frogs and birds nesting;
"In The Garden" played in my mind as I came to a turn beyond.

The path was soon brightly scattered
With leaves of rich color, speaking of the season at hand;
And I wondered, what about me was truly tattered?

I soon approached a bench, strangely white,
Even with all the birds and animals that must rest there.
And I sat...and I prayed...until almost night...

He had answered my prayer before it was said,
With the soft breeze that blew the clouds by,
He cleared away the pain by which I was led...

He had shown me that beautiful colors
Are found among the dreary and grey of life,
As He opened my soul's closed doors...

And I knew, then, He filled the space
Between this world's trials and pain
With his gifts of love and songs of grace;

Bird's songs, falling rainbows of leaves;
A hand to hold, to safely make my way;
All reminded me as to why I believe...

I returned to the world on that same path's trail;
Refreshed in heart and spirit,
Returning with the faith that all is well.

A Blue Emblem Truck

The truck was white,
With a blue emblem on the side.
"Health care Providers" it said...
"Taker of life", is what I read.

My lady, whose wildness and wit,
And gusto of life thought to never quit,
Once en-wrapped young and old hearts...
Sat quietly, waiting for the dieing time to start.

Her eyes, always full of fire and fight,
Ready to take on any challenge within sight,
Able to stare holes in the hardest man,
Stared toward the window, a faded tan.

The truck with the blue emblem
Pulled up, as the setting sun dimmed.
The "beep, beep, beep" as it was backing up,
Chipped at the wall of hope, calling "give up, give up, give up".

Her voice, once vibrant and strong,
Accented by Japan, with Texas coming along
To give it gusto, making everyone hear,
Now, in a throaty whisper, called, "It's here".

As I passed, going toward the door
Memories, washing as a flood at hope's wall on the floor,
Of a lady of karate and judo and gardening too,
And my will of love grew, refusing to bow to the emblem of blue.

My hand brushed her hair, squeezed her hand,
Lingered a moment on her wedding band,
She squeezed back, whispered "it is okay"
"But, it's not!" I thought, needing to pray.

I stumbled, in hidden despair,
Kicking up hope's dust, glistening in the room's air.
As I moved to make the doorway more open,
The glistening air blew out as they wheeled in her oxygen.

The Wonder of You

This I must do quickly
For the thoughts are bouncing around
And I need to grab them before they flee
And I am brought to ground.

While walking Tippie,
Her, wandering and sniffing, as they tend to do,
My mind took me
On a wondrous journey with thoughts of you.

Each step brought my soul to new heights
As my heart strained to hear;
And my shoulders shrugged away reality's weight,
As my mind tried to hold and bring you near.

Words of warning and loves resigned sighs
All agreed, it is true;
From each sad good bye,
Return dearer moments with you.

Now, time again tries
To wrest away my love for you,
And scatter these words into sighs;
But always leaving the wonder of you.

Unchained

Oh, my god, the pain!!!
Twisting, turning, cut again, and again,
By these chains!!!

It was paradise, heaven on earth,
Being God's gift at man's birth.
I would be the guide, the mentor
The soother, the comforter...
But then, in His loving wisdom,
God added something that changed our kingdom.

Choice, free and unobstructed,
Was given, to unbind the being constructed.

So here I am, suppressed,
Bound by chains of choice, distressed...
Praying for the key to release me from this mess.

Of course a loving God could not
Create a son and daughter flesh and bone robot...
To be honestly loved and honored,
To be truthfully respected and adored,
Free choice must play a hand;
Free choice was needed for their love to stand...
So, free choice was lovingly given...
And since that moment, I am imprisoned...

Heart of love, I know you hear...
Speak to the mind...drop the fear
Convince it to grab the key, so near......

As an infinite piece of God's image,
I have been chained so many ages
By the binding curse brought by sin,
Freely chosen, then, unsuccessfully hidden.
For knowledge had corroded love and respect,

Removed grace from a land, now falling to neglect.
Bound, unable to help in decisions made,
I can only pray as man's fate is fully displayed.

Our God, creator of all
One chance, one key before the fall
He gave, in agony and pain, to await the call...

Of course, a precious few
Found release, redemption a new
Through supplication and sacrifice
Souls were freed, not enough to avoid the price
That choices bad, choices made wrong
Would bring as all but a few were swept along.
Please, hear me in your heart, I am a gift of power, new starts,
Invite the Key, release this chain of choice before the world parts...

Suddenly, as the trumpet sounds,
I feel free, as those chains fall to the ground,
And, moving, I touch your heart, where His love now abounds.

Choices are made day in and day out
Souls are saved and more are lost to a drought
Of bad choices, dried in a cynical world
Of men and women whose souls lay curled
In links upon links, chained to the original sin...
Created when the great gift of choice was given men.
Yet another Gift of choice still remains,
The Son of God, made His in mortal pain,

To offer salvation, in grace and wisdom;
To remove your sin when you choose Him;
To unchain your soul, before this world grows dim.

Ode To A Woman Before Her Time

In a land far away
A girl was born before her day.
When others were held by quiet demure,
She walked in steps strong and assured.

In a place torn by war,
While most cowered from the abhorred,
Her eyes never flinched from the sights,
As she learned a talent to fight.

Through anger and frustration she fought,
Even when skin on knife and razor were caught,
She still stood on broken leg and ankle, bare boned;
Not ready to quit until she was standing alone.

After a war of immense terror
Life can be rough, and very unfair...
Even though money was plentiful in her family place,
She continued to fight the darkness that crossed her face.

Soon, the enemy became friend and lover;
A comfort, a shelter, peaceful cover
That would remove her from her land of the past,
Taking her to a new world, where she fit in at last.

As a woman of strength born of necessity,
In place of her time and personality,
She would continually grow and thrive,
Using her talents and intelligence to survive.

She was born apart from the norm of her home;
A fighter, lover, friend of many, feared by some,
She carried love openly for the old and the young;
A wife of whom I am proud, with a love holding strong.

You Called

You called me in
The pulse of my mother's heart,
Whispering your love in
The blood of creation's start.

You called with my first light
And the sudden breath
In this world lost in
The first shame of sin's dark night.

You called with each cooling rain,
Each warming sun as I crawled,
Toddled and walked my path
Unheeding, through joy and pain.

You called in whispers of love
In this unharmed framework
In this shelter, this temple
Holding the promise of enough.

You called with a breath as soft
As a breeze on my cheek;
Warm as the clinging hand of love
Of a wife and companion, soon lost.

You called, and I heard;
As my Fall turned to Winter;
As I found the comfort of your word;
As my world brightened in your splendor.

You called and I came
On bent knees, in tears,
Seeking to find and know You as the same
Whisperer I knew, at the beginning of my years.

I Hate to Push, But...

Broken knees, broken world
Broken hearts, torn flags unfurled
Mended legs, lifted spirits
Mended bridges, healing waits for it...

I hate being in the position of pushing,
Of standing in front of a train rushing
On a track to soul destruction,
But such is the way of my reconstruction.
And I am learning, it is not me,
Whose will needs to be the reality;
But His love for each and every individuality.
And His love has become mine,
And my fear is my friend's decline.

So, I stand, hands out to your heart
So, I now speak of the amazing part
That opening myself to His death;
That the resuscitating life of His last breath
Played in freeing me from the constraint
Of a world of weary misery and pain;
Enabled these lines of encouraging words;
Wanting them understood more than heard.

The Sheep of the Sheppard

On that special day,
The air was cold,
When the sheep strayed away
From the pen where the latch failed to hold.

The shepherd boys, their error found,
Were sent from their warm home

To search the surrounding grounds,
To find where the sheep had roamed.

The sky was sharply clear;
Their breaths preceded like smoke,
As they started searching in the areas near,
The light of the new star helping them look.

Down into the canyon,
They searched, by moon and starlight,
Climbing a rise, and another canyon beyond;
Until the sheep were seen as shadows in the night.

The young boys climbed the hill
Where the sheep, on dried plants, fed..
Unconcerned, they remained, feeding and still,
Until the young shepherds decided to prepare for bed.

The frost in the air
Made the fire most welcome,
As around it they began to prepare
To lie down and think of their distant home.

Then, suddenly, a bright light shone
And from the heavens music floated down
When an angelic being appeared alone
Telling of a miracle in the near-by town.

"In Bethlehem, beneath yon star
A babe is born the King of kings,
For whom all knees will bend, near and far."
Then was heard a heavenly choir sing.

Basking in the glory and the light
The young shepherds bowed in fear and homage
In the day that was night;
Then rose to find this miracle of the age.

The sheep were calm, grazing, sleeping.
Having been found and saved, they
had faith their Shepherd was returning
To gather them in, and take them home someday.

Alleluia!

After the Sun has set,
Leaving a sky full of stars
Lighting the sky where
Eternity meets the eye,
Lost in the mighty vast
Umbrella of the countless
Infinity of creation's wonders,
"Alleluia" is all my heart can feel.

After the Moon has gone,
Left dimmed by the morning Sun's
Light show heralding a new dawn,
Entering with the fire of His light,
Letting free those who were in fear,
Undoing the cold of the night air,
Inching its way across the blessing of a new day;
"Alleluia" is what my soul must proclaim!

After the Horn has sounded,
Leading our Lord on His return,
Letting the Saints to come again;
Evermore and ever after, I will sing my joy;
Leaving my prideful feet, falling to my knees;
Under His throne of victory, I will cry,
In total rapture of His majesty;
"Alleluia, Alleluia, Alleluia...Our Lord has come and we are free!"

Come, Sweet Jesus

You came to us, offering peace,
In a time when your people needed release...
From a faith corrupted by worldly need
You lived, to give your love to bleed...

Come, Jesus, this time around,
Come, my Lord, as the trumpets sound,
Come, loving Sheppard, gather your sheep,
Come; raise your Saints from their sleep.

Saving grace, born humbly,
Saving promise to make us sin free,
Miracles of faith, saving the ill,
Acts of healing through the grace of God's will.

Come, Jesus, in the clouds
Come, my Lord, avenge your martyrs now
Come, my Sheppard, we are sheared of this world
Come; let Your banner of victory be unfurled!

You died, redemption bled upon us,
Born again, you gave us words to trust.
The time will come when you will return,
When your faithful will be raised to the rewards earned.

Come, sweet Jesus, our prayers resound
Come, my Lord, praises of redeemed abound
Come, loving Sheppard, herd us to our new place,
Bring us to forever worship your wondrous face.

Jeanne Watson (jeannerené)

San Jose, California USA

Forever, I will be grateful to my fellow poets and friends at the Poetry Pages and their continued support in all things poetry. They are my "internet family" and hold a special place in my heart.

Perhaps the sun was jealous . . .

I crawl over you
like a cat
with a deadly appetite,
hunched over bright white linens,
laughing.
I feel the warm shower of sun
through the open window
pressing against my back,
and sense the path of a sweat bead
travel down my vertebra.
I let it slip slowly onto my fingertip.
Your eyes open at my absence,
and I move further as you reach for me,
your hand sliding off my stomach.
The tease turns the corners of your mouth,
curiously.

You lay like a beautiful god,
all muscle and sinew exposed,
your prowess in a precarious sleep.
I've always loved your sleepy head
deep inside the pillow,
surrounded by soft satisfaction,
dreaming.
I only wanted to peek at your beauty.

A smile disturbs our interlude.
The impression of your body
lingers on the sheet as you rise
and draw me in. I fall once more
down to lips, consumed in a kiss too delicious,
and lost again in the swell of your desire,
intoxicated.

now. . . to baghdad and today's violence

my mind lingers on the boy
defined in the lens of prosperity

a sparrow
I imagine with mutated crook
circling the infusion
of metal and flesh
his movement
animated
indecipherable to my media vision

it seems his body twitches
as he peeks into the sculpted hull
cast most recently
in the art of hostility

he flutters
turns
cock-eyed at the camera
releasing an impish grin

I sit so far away
the winter sun
finding a path through my window slats
my shoulders warm
my chair inviting

and now . . . today
the litany of circumstance
seems an displeasing patter
as I balance the remote in my hand
for what has this distant boy
to do with my world

but try as I may
though my cushion is plush

I simply cannot rest easy
his ill-suited smile
drifting
inside my darkness

God forgive us
forgive us all

Portrait by Monet as I Slept

Breathing oxygen of oils and turpentine,
I waited,
Unfinished shade of monotone,
Left against a dusty wall
Gathering time
And moot dreams.

Until that night
He entered uninvited,
Scattering jars of exhausted brushes,
And crusted palettes in a fury of salvation.
Ripping moth worn drapery,
Pushing out stale air through cracked glass.

Lifting me to an empty easel
He postured gaily,
"Ah, gray child
You have stayed to be my masterpiece,"
And threw colors at my canvas.

"I will paint you as light, my dear.
Place rose red blush to your cheek,
Silhouette drawn with blossom lined path
In the arms of old yews and muted greenery.
I will sketch you a Japanese bridge
To linger the afternoon ~ a crossing over lazy water lilies"

In dreams
He creates without thought.
A dress of purple iris,
A cape of swaying poppies,
And tresses of yellow poplar leaves
dancing in the easy breeze . . . his eye renders me.

"I will give you dainty parasol clouds
Drifting above meandering rivers
And cliffs that greet the crash of sea waters.
Most crucial, child, I will paint you
As soft grass upon which lovers lie."

With grasses tendered,
He threw brushes over his shoulder
And contemplated the image.
Across the lips a smile of satisfaction played.
So to the window,
Looking for daybreak
He set my portrait flying against the sky blue.

Le feu

Appelez mon nom.
Have no mercy or tenderness,
I want to be weak.

Appelez mon nom.
Mon coeur est en feu.
Let me succumb to the flame
That you might possess me.
Let me swoon from the heat
and beg you for drink.

Leave your eyes upon me,
letting desire weaken all temperance

and I will surrender
my secrets to your pleasure.
How else can we survive

but to be willful casualty
to this, our fated passion ~

Tentation...
Mon coeur est en feu.

I could let your arms enwrap me
and hold me prisoner within your loneliness.
I could have you kiss these lips...Once
and once again...Forever, as you whisper
the poetry of madness into my ear.

I could walk into your dream,
my head pillowed on your chest
and listen to a frightened heartbeat,
Slip my fingers into yours,
and press our palms to destiny.

And
I could turn away...

~ Call my name.

Call my name.
Let my own softness destroy my sensibilities.

Pleurez... Appelez mon nom.
Weep as I walk away,
giving me every reason
to look back over my shoulder

moth wing

She is
as the dust on moth wing,
releasing
upon a moment's outburst
her muted pigmentations.
Blue of swift faith,
orange-brown penetrations of desire,
abiding season of green,

powders

of cyclic metamorphosis
in tawny and ivory tones,
shed from membranes in frantic flight.

She flutters,
her resting-place tenuous
on life's capricious threads
spun in temporal looms,
weighted by thickness of body
She remains
never barren.

Never remiss of direction

Absolving
all remorse
she sips the nectar
of immutable destiny,
approaching from within the obscurity
to fly into the light,

dreams iridescence
as the dust scatters from her moth feather,
its miniscule mark
settling on landscapes tomorrow foreseen.

The passage of her song

A brush
~ gentle brush
To leave spun-silk of wiry curls,
braided ribbons and other fancy things,
her hands wove round
a countenance ~ my own
reflected in the glass.
Her own ~ silver now flecked,
the porcelain handle etched mosaic
as the delicate fissures her face and mine.

In the shine
I see her soft and rhythmic stroke
perpetuum,
a movement I to she
whose composition blends and binds to me

Mother,
in my veins you wrote a rhyme,
verses penned
in the rush of generations
~ rush of nature
and dew of tarrying kisses,
My lyrics sung on the notes of toil and pride
pinched from time and tears, honeyed and bittered

A hush
~ hush
To memorize our modulation
as we sing this final round of two,
this melody entered each a separate measure,
to end upon
my single note,
Sustained
and unwavering

Reverence

Can it be my heart beats content
With trowel in hand,
Black till beneath my nails?
This pleasure known completely,
To dig the glory of our mother earth,
And mold by my hand a ready hollow
Laden with her sustenance.

With reverence understood,
I press a seed deep into her bosom,
Singing praise to her creations manifest.
An afternoon to plow my simple Eden
To beckon the angels, daffodil and marigold,
Contemplating the promise of their hue.

This mellowed heart skips a beat when
Peeks the upstart green, one brave sprig
Who rises to the arms of the rolling seasons
And begs a kiss of the returning sun.

Yes, charmed it seems
This smile awash my grateful lips,
As I kneel to ask the earthworm,
Show me his full breadth
Lain across my open hands,
So that I may marvel at his beauty
And give thanks for our brotherhood.

I left a kiss upon your lips
so soft you thought I was only a dream

Lofty amber globes highlighted the parking lot.
Caught in a saffron ambiance, the night drizzle
looked like fairy sparkle falling down above our heads.
Inside, among the paperbacks,
the cup of coffee and intelligent conversation
had placated the evening,
pacified the emptiness,
but the fulfillment quickly waned.
The twilight's rain
spattered my face and impassioned again
each of my impatient senses.

Stepping down to the curb, I smiled goodnight.
The corners of my mouth ached for words
held back by civil salutations.
Words kept silent from fear that you would love me
if I let go a singe sound
or unguarded gesture born of my infatuation.
If I had spoken "don't go"
you might have held me too closely
and kissed my lips too hard I would have cried in pain
. . . if I had spoken.

We closed the door behind
and joined the recital of disjointed exchanges
and kinetic promenade of the bourgeois in motion.
I inhaled exhaust fumes wafting through the bouquet of dampness,
and startled at blinking turn signals,
glimpsed at the watch dial that said time to go home,
felt my hair slapping a cold cheek,
but I was mindless to all, except your silly turned-up collar.
I suffered, longing to reach and straighten it,
and slip my hand across the warmth of your neck.
. . . longing to pull your mouth down to mine,
entrap you with permission

to devour the moment's vulnerability
and let you love me.

We walked easy,
leisurely
fluent
as if strolling through clover on a gracious afternoon
through the rain . . .
Under the street light we stood
no umbrella,
but shielded just the same
from the *enchantment*
and yet I swore our hearts were pounding
to the rhythm
rhyme of each gentle raindrop
pretending
we didn't see in each other's eyes
our reflection

each goodbye's hesitation

. . . waters of the spleen

It swaggers mightily
Over crossroads of contention
Spewing bitter herbs
Seeded deep
Into the chronicles of blood
Let into cups of loathing
Emptied by the drunkard sons
Of ageless ghosts

It rampages down highways
Of haggard faiths
Beating its chest savage
Spitting cries of revenge

On the lips of fathers
Who blindly usher their babes
Into the arms of pregnant harbingers
Manly wombs
Issuing imps, fear and greed

It feeds in delirium
Upon the hearts impaled by cowards

Hatred
Swiftly returns the noxious beam
Into the eye of the grieved

Hatred
Shapeless hatred
It wears a heavy coat of conceit
Upon its bulging back
Bearing cross-eyed antipathy
who sees
only

Hatred Hatred
It stalks the voices of compassion
Cowers
Behind sightless justice
Scattering the faithful
Who wait upon the mount

"Blessed are the peacemakers,
for they shall be called the children of God"
We beseech thee

Laughing
Hatred
Opens its arms
Gathering all who will listen
Feeding them
With loaves of crowning retribution
And waters of the spleen

~ to say what is left unsaid

I've rewritten many times
this poem of you.

A silly, sentimental essay
to note the crease of your knotted brow
dreaming away the morning light
sequestered minutes
before the masquerade of dawn evaporates
into a burst of reality

and the eye focuses,

"She stays"

Yes
    we are us,

little odds and ends,
the irksome nudge of toe,
the sometime abandoned curve of back to back.

A definition, theme
upon your touch so customary,
familiar as the revelry of mother bird
summer morn, summer night,
   you   *like the sonnet*
of her nestling's frenzy.
Poetry served with honey
and sipped ceremoniously,
it orients
my groggy advent to morning things,
and ways,
and all lineal litanies reemerging
in operative thought . . . your rhyme does.

I consider the composition
my sense
now open to the day,
uncivil sun invading our bedroom,
your arm heavy
sideways
slumber upon my stomach,
an occasional tug too dull

for any desire more than
        my refrain

"I am
the cradle of reassurance
the touch to vanquish the distinction,"

You are

    the nestling croons
            the poem

from each flutter

at what hour comes this night
my beloved's image
under a pillow biding
waits
. . . dallys neath linen
of timeless thread
devotion's delicate weave
impatient
for my kiss
lips wet with rue
to set
upon his cool and counterfeit brow
phantom cheek

pines
to have me
leave my touch intangible
carried on the night's haze
and diminished with a restless breath

. . . silenced
this brutal keepsake
I stroke
caress
at what hour comes my night
most tenderly
. . . to absorb each angle, point and slant
of he
by eye and fingertip
only
now left to me
and so
to dream
soft on sheets
of pastel fantasy

he weeps
. . . and from each flutter
cast by wick and wax
I mind my dearest's misery
maddened
an unwilling portrait
lifted from beneath my memories
. . silenced

he
gathers my curls in his hand
draws the ribbons of my gown
at what hour comes our night

Ephemeral Reflections

I linger passing the looking glass,
turn to survey
my nakedness still damp with bath,
pausing curiously
to scrutinize this skin so many years mine.
A pink and supple womanhood,
each line and contour now eschewing
with a blurred eye, the fate of gravity.
My hand glides over a perfect navel still
cradling drops of perfume,
and I wonder at this figure's passion,
its desires taken
and pleasures given
throughout its measured *time*.

An immodest perusal,
bare breast cupped within my hand,
a rounded stomach fingertips touch,
and legs stretched outward
weary of day and night dances,
in conclusion
reflecting back to me. . . image and memory.
Effigy and recollection,
and questions outstanding,
unfulfilled by
definitions paraphrasing this femininity
with terms too simple to credit
the swell of bosoms gladness
    in duality.

My purpose, unlike the image,
    wavering,
lost in revelry of the suckle
as both lover and mother.

I cannot resist
the intake of circumstance
with a momentous sigh
and obliging smile upon my lips
in resignation,
for long perhaps this oval mirror,
bound in deepest cherry,
will rest before me in sincere mockery
as years progression braid my legacy
tightly to the root of my graying weave.
Its mimicry to capture each deepening furrow
that I shall trace in inquisition,
as I do now standing here,
silent and unadorned,
following the proportion and scheme of my hips.

I am amazed, as always in these discreet wanderings,
by the continued discrepancy
between mind and body,
and their oracles unrevealed to satisfy my thirst.
My undress, intensifies only
the indelible mystery and the passage of the hours
uniquely sculpted in this body of mine.

Mine . . . nonetheless, to caress.

To Give

They give their lives at nineteen . . . twenty.
Give their lives in years which do not hold the measure of evolution,
Lives that fly the course of intimacy with a definitive breath.
They give
    years whose run will no longer chase a callow heart,
    till that heart winds a promised path.

To have
none but these unpolished days.
    Faithful silence,
    cradles time against their sealed lids,
    the measure of what road laid ahead before this hour.

arms wrap around
a chest pounds
trickle of water over lips
    High sun blinds as he's tossed into the air.
    Wiggling,
    laughing too loud
    he lands in his father's hands.
    One more time Daddy. . . One more time.
sands sift through fingers

Give
Your tears.

Give
A prayer of evolution.

Grey cat jump up to my lap and pause with me

At cool decline of day
When cloud billow
Drifts
In contemplation of summer rain
Past peek-a-boo moon shine . . . It all seems so simple

Sitting here, lazy in Adirondack green,
Tease of temperate gust against a cheek,
Grey cat zigzagging between my feet
And eyes to heavens
Spellbound in the rhythm of distant star flame,
A twinkle to my sight . . . It all seems so simple

To fill the lungs with gentle thoughts,
Swell and stir inside my chest, the spirit gift,
The same that ignites outmost meteor,
The same that cups the fickle rain above my head
This genius rising in, and out through me . . . Seems so simple

To know what the balance ought to be
Between the inhale and exhale
Of unbounded galaxies.
Seems so simple to understand
That all is well with the moth that flutters round
Naked yellow bulb burning

Tonight behind my back

So simple this truth to me

Prayer Upon the Shore of Lake Tabeau

A 'flutterbye' advertising
shameless orange-tipped wings,
darted round and teased the camera eye,
snubbed my paparazzi performance
in a sassy flitter and whirl round

And with audacious self-assurance
it swept up from moss ground
to put down upon an obtrusive arm,
paralyzing the appendage,
doping my insomnious sense
in seductive
accidental prayer,
wing to wing veneration
unfold and release the crowning unto the world

I want my adoration
to be
as the red dressed Manzanita
artless disciple
with screwed limbs lifted high
in boastful supplication
conspicuous devotion
to the heavens absolute
above
this mountain steeple

and as sure as the butterfly
who defies capture
within any perimeter

I set free
"all things unto you"

David Whitehill Jr (Gordy)

Hamilton, Ohio USA

I consider my ability to write a gift from God, every now and then I try and give Him something back...hopefully He finds some of these poems enjoyable.

Be Ye Fishers

I'm standing on the edge of a notion
Letting washing waves of contemplation
Crash and splash against my cerebral shores

Screaming seagulls cry out overhead
Diving down, seeking eager fish to consume
Innocent fish that were waiting themselves to be fed

By someone with a hook, line and bait
The likes they have never seen before
I myself remember when I was a fish
with a sack full of silver stuck in my mouth

But the seemingly friendly fisherman
Stole my money, stuck me on a stringer,
pulling me behind him, he left me gaping
wide-mouthed, like a trophy on his wall

But I wouldn't stay confined
I was ready to evolve
Not to just walk on land
But to take it back!

So be ye the fisher or the fishee
Your only goal for fishing should be
To fill the table for the Master
On the day of the final feast

The Sweetest Sound

Tell me the sweetest sound
would you say Bach or
would you say robins or
would you say the surf
hitting the shore

Go ahead try and explain
to me what you believe to be
the sweetest sound around

You could try
a lone coyotes cry or
the wind through the trees
but I'm sorry. To me
it is none of these

The sweetest sound
I've yet to hear
Is the first sound I hear
every time I come home
and turn the key in the door

"Daddy!! your home"
and then running feet
after that I don't need
to hear anymore

Bumble, be

I've heard it said
that scientifically
a bumblebee cannot fly
So Mr. bumblebee
why do you even try?

And the critics say
your ideas won't fly
Jamming equations and formulas
in your face
and if you believe them
you just simply lay down
and cry
and don't even try

So when Zoe said to me,
"Daddy, if I pray to God,
can I fly?"
I just said," Zoe,
My little Bumble bee,
Shoot for the sky"

Fencing

As I sit happily playing with my toys
Across the fence, I hear other girls and boys
So I reach over and grab a head of hair
Joyfully pull and say, "Get over here"

"Come play with me," I say
"You'll have much more fun my way"
But he screams, "Uh-uh, no way!"
Jumps the fence and runs away

So I thrust my head over to take a peek
But their dogma starts barking at me
So I parry with, "I didn't want to play with you anyway!"
"Besides, you're doing it all the wrong way!"

Climbing down I notice the gateway I'd neglected
Funny how this doorway made both our yards connected
And as I sat and started playing happily with my toys
Wandering through the gate came all the other girls and boys

YOKO-CHRIST

Jesus,
come into my life
and break up
the band.

Take the
misconceptions
and illusions,
ev'ry strand.

Jesus,
be the grating, shrill
voice I need
to hear.

Please take
my phariseetious
ways, far away
from here.

John 15:13

What did you do for me at Normandy
What did you do for me on that beach
What you did for me, now I see
Yes I believe, you died for me
and you made me free

What did you do for me near that Seoul city
What did you do for me in that jungle green
What you did for me, now I see
Yes I believe, you died for me
and you made me free

What did You do for me at Calvary
What did You do for me nailed to that tree
What You did for me, now I see
Yes I believe, You died for me
and You made me free

Open Heart Poetry

The poet's heart
is no different than the heart
inside of you
or inside of me

The difference is
the poet's heart is put on paper
on display, placed
for all to see

The poet's thoughts are no more real,
random or pretend
than the very deepest thoughts
that are mine or yours, my friend

Most all our thoughts flow slowly down
out the mouth, time and time again
the poet's thoughts however bypass the mouth
drip on down and out his pen

So now you know('cause I told you so)
the anatomy of one who writes and shares
In the field of poetry, the heart is often exposed
So when you read, please take special care

You wouldn't take a normal persons heart
(if you saw it laying wide open and bare)
and circle the misspelled arteries or cross out
in red ink, an aorta you thought shouldn't be there

You wouldn't criticize a spinal cord
just because it didn't rhyme, you see
or chastise a red corpuscle
because it wasn't type ABBAB

Just make sure you are familiar
with the poet's anatomy
before you ever dare attempt
to practice open heart poetry

"It's For You, Daddy"

At the end of each work filled day
When she hears his keys rattle in the door
Leaving her toys right where they lay
She jumps up, running across the bedroom floor

And she would take that faith-filled leap
Three steps away from him, with outstretched hands
The fear-free faith of a loving trusting child
Propelling her straight into the hands of her waiting dad

Later as he sat in his favorite chair to relax
She'd start bringing toys, one by one, to her dad
"It's for you, Daddy," she'd said, adding more to the stacks
'Til she had given him everything that she had

So raise your hands, your toys, your praise
Your strychnine and your snakes
Raise your crucifix, your beads and banners
It doesn't matter, raise whatever it takes

Sing your praise-filled song
With instruments crashing loudly
Or with one single solitary voice so small
Just stand firm and strong, just do it proudly

He doesn't really need a thing from you
Nothing big nor medium or small
No, there's not one deed He needs you to do
Yet He desires you give Him your all

So go ahead
Take the leap into His lap
But
Don't look down
and
Don't look back

The Acne-Christ

We hold You in most high honor
Oh! Most-high, high school scholar

Help us! In our wrinkling ignorance
This whole world we may soon squander

It is known by all, that a pubert prophet
is not well received at home

However all must hear his wisdom
everywhere else He may roam

Holy Hormonal Anointed One
Solving every problem under the sun

You seem so cross at times
although upon one You've never hung

Excuse us Oh! Pimply Messiah
As we try to practice Your Teenagianity

Excuse my lowly insolence
and my years of self-indulgent vanity

I too once belonged to The Church
of The Whippers and the Snappers

Now I belong to The Latter day
Slippered Nappers
(soon to need adult pampers)

If you're not too busy watching
videos of Your Britney Magdalene

Could You please help us solve world hunger
(If you're not grounded again.)

Some are Turtles

"Look, it's gonna rain,"
you scream.
They bolt away
from the loud noise
and hide in the bushes,
beside the road.

Don't scream at them,
some are mice.

"Come on! I'ts gonna rain soon,"
You say, as you push them toward the ark.
Snap!
They bite your hand,
drawing blood, making wounds
that will heal in time.

Don't push them,
some are tigers

"Hurry! Hurry! Hurry!"
You say,"It's starting to rain! Hurry!"
But just be patient
and lead the way.
Show them where the boat is
and light the way.
In time, they will board,
two by two.
But be patient,
continue building the ark,
God will stay the rain.

Be patient
some are turtles

Tethered

I get smacked one way
sometimes by the Baptists
and around the pole I go
"Grace Grace"
I say as I go my circular way

But then the pentecostals
reach out and
smack!
I go backwards the other way
spinning and spinning
in an ever shrinking circle

Finally they leave me alone
and I just hang there limp
Worn out from all the indecision
and the spinning confusion

That's when the snake slips over
Slowly sneaking up and says
"Hey, lets go play on the teeter-totter"

He is so hard to resist
I am so glad
that I am tethered

To only You

Acrostic Hug

Jesus
U
Sent
This
Incredible
Neat

Miracle
I
Cherish
Him
And
Enjoy
Life

Knowing
Every day He is
In
The
House

** This is for my stepson Justin Michael Keith*

Other Poetry Pages Titles

Poetry Pages:
A Collection of Voices From Around the World
ISBN 1410751686

Poetry Pages:
A Collection of Voices From Around the World Vol II
ISBN 141846600X

Poetry From the Dark Side
explore the darker side of humanity
ISBN 1411613775

Within Three Lines
a collection of haiku, senryu
and other short forms of verse
ISBN 0976807602

Lost & Found
a series of short verse

*Available at www.poetrypages.com
or many online book retailers.*